Praise for *Reality in Ruins*

"An eye-opening, a must-read book for our time, a time marked by what Jared calls the Disreality of our making. *Reality in Ruins* identifies our blind spots, whether the reader is a conservative or liberal, or dispossessed and numb, all breathing in the culture war fumes. In order to remove the toxins in our cultural soil, we need to be truly set free by Jesus's greater love and truth, and we need a guidebook and map toward future thriving—Jared provides exactly that in this illuminating book."

—Makoto Fujimura, artist and author of
Art Is and *Culture Care*

"In this era of disreality and conspiracy, we must all think deeply and purposefully about the forces shaping how we experience the world around us. *Reality in Ruins* is just the book for this journey. As Christian nationalism continues to dominate our existence, Jared shows us how to be claimed by the truth instead of always trying to wield a twisted version of it. Only then can we begin to tell a better story, one marked by love and liberation."

—Andrew Whitehead, scholar and award-winning
author of *American Idolatry*

"Jared Stacy is an eminently trustworthy voice on conspiracism within American evangelicalism. He brings to the topic a rare combination of expertise, empathy, and lived experience. *Reality in Ruins* will challenge, enlighten, and encourage readers from across the political and religious spectrums. This is not only a timely book, but it is an urgently needed one."

—Karen Swallow Prior, author of
The Evangelical Imagination

"Written with both compassion and hard-won experience, *Reality in Ruins* delves deep into the crisis of 'holy paranoia' that has gripped an increasingly large part of evangelical Christianity in America over the last century. Having been part of this world, Jared Stacy innately grasps how conspiracy theories and extremism offer both false hope and false idols to their evangelical believers. This is a vitally important book about a subject that has invited a great deal of media sneering and liberal derision, but little in the way of understanding or empathy."

—Mike Rothschild, journalist and author of *Jewish Space Lasers*

"Jared Stacy wants to let you in on a secret: at least since the Great Awakening, American Protestants have had a deforming affair with conspiratorial thinking. The historical story he has to tell is one that every American who identifies as an evangelical should know. But what is truly groundbreaking is the fearless gospel he offers his readers as a theological alternative."

—Dr. Brian Brock, professor of theology, University of Aberdeen

"Much ink has been spilled on the ways MAGA's religious project has damaged American political life, but *Reality in Ruins* shows us how it has blighted American Christianity. In this acute yet heartfelt work, Jared Stacy grounds his story in his experience as a pastor who has resisted disinformation and discord, and offers a path to redeem the faith as well as the nation."

—Anne Nelson, award-winning author of *Shadow Network* and lecturer on human rights

REALITY IN RUINS

REALITY IN RUINS

HOW CONSPIRACY THEORY
BECAME AN AMERICAN
EVANGELICAL CRISIS

JARED STACY, PhD

HarperOne
An Imprint of HarperCollinsPublishers

Without limiting the exclusive rights of any author, contributor or the publisher of this publication, any unauthorized use of this publication to train generative artificial intelligence (AI) technologies is expressly prohibited. HarperCollins also exercise their rights under Article 4(3) of the Digital Single Market Directive 2019/790 and expressly reserve this publication from the text and data mining exception.

REALITY IN RUINS. Copyright © 2026 by Jared Stacy. All rights reserved. No part of this book may be used or reproduced in any manner whatsoever without written permission except in the case of brief quotations embodied in critical articles and reviews. For information, address HarperCollins Publishers, 195 Broadway, New York, NY 10007. In Europe, HarperCollins Publishers, Macken House, 39/40 Mayor Street Upper, Dublin 1, D01 C9W8, Ireland.

HarperCollins books may be purchased for educational, business, or sales promotional use. For information, please email the Special Markets Department at SPsales@harpercollins.com.

hc.com

FIRST EDITION

Designed by Jason Kayser

Library of Congress Cataloging-in-Publication Data has been applied for.

ISBN 978-0-06-345375-3

Printed in the United States of America

26 27 28 29 30 LBC 5 4 3 2 1

For Stevie

**Human kind
Cannot bear very much reality.**

—T. S. Eliot, "Burnt Norton," *Four Quartets*

CONTENTS

Introduction 1

1 Pain, Panic, and Power 7
2 Power of Story 41
3 An Untold Story 69
4 The Plot Devices of Holy Paranoia 126
5 Red-Pilled Evangelicalism 161
6 Claimed by Reality 183
7 Toward a Common World 211
8 Sand in the Machine 252

Acknowledgments 275

Notes 277

INTRODUCTION

Conspiracy theory and evangelical Christianity in America run together. They always have. This bitter entanglement creates a crisis of fact *and* faith. The book you're holding explores how this crisis came to be. In this sense, it's descriptive—naming the pain many of us feel and recounting a history long forgotten.

But the book is also prescriptive. Knowledge demands responsibility. This is an invitation to look back for those who are trying to look ahead, to find a way forward through the raging torrent of conspiracism in the now.

Many have never entered an evangelical church or institution. But the crisis of conspiracism in evangelicalism has consequences beyond itself. These consequences are now painfully clear. And those with courage to confront these consequences will pay a cost.

But the cost for a better future can be paid in confidence. Reality might be in ruins, but we can do our part to work toward a common world again. This book is meant to provide trail markers for our way toward that common world, one revealed by better stories, against the tide of unmoored, anxious suspicion.

HOW TO READ THIS BOOK

Admittedly, this isn't a reference book. It's not filled with techniques or tips for winning arguments with friends. It offers little ammo toward shattering the illusions of family members or friends captive to conspiracism.

So if you're reading to *win*, you've already lost. This book is for those who know the agonizing alchemy of pain and panic created by conspiracy theory and are looking for a solid place to stand and people to join.

This book is for those who want to resist the power our clashing realities wields. Not just at the level of national politics, mass movements, and ideological causes. But also, and especially so, at the level of everyday life. I'm talking about the pain of those whose lives bear the scars of silences, of separation, all wrought by the conspiratorial, supercharged by Christian faith.

With this costly fracturing in mind, this is a book meant to help us remember what it means to tell the truth in a time when we are bearing the cost of so much untruth. This book testifies to the better stories, the uncomfortable facts that sit with us—sometimes for years—before we change. It makes this point from several different approaches: history, theology, culture, and ethics. But it's personal, too. You see, I was an evangelical.

And so this isn't a book about conspiracism in general. This is a book about conspiracism as it manifests within evangelical Christian communities, churches, and institutions. Places where I spent my childhood, where I studied, where I served. From the wood-paneled walls of a church sanctuary, to the Sunday school sandwich cookies, that was my life. I know the taste of that watered-down pink lemonade in fellowship halls. I've pastored in those converted warehouse churches and studied in the seminary libraries that smelled of old books. These spaces were shared with a people who, for better or worse, have forever played a part in shaping my life.

Studies show that, during the pandemic and the election of 2020, evangelical Christians—my people—were one of the highest religious communities to traffic in conspiratorial beliefs about COVID and Trump's stolen election conspiracy.[1] These statistics preview an untold history of the conspiratorial gospel at the heart of evangelicalism. But whenever history seems too abstract or distant, I want us to remember this conspiratorial gospel carries an intimate cost, one of pain and even trauma.[2]

It would be an exhaustive impossibility to counter every conspiracy theory, to trace every claim and connect the dots. After all, they change every day. Instead, what I hope to do is sketch some hopeful and helpful answers for those who are left with questions like "How did we get here?" or "Is there a way forward?"

Most of all, I want to reflect on what it means to tell the truth. I do this as a practicing Christian. But also as an apostate from the nationalist and militant Christianity in ascendancy across the United States. This Christianity uses the name of Jesus to sanction authoritarian politics in the pursuit of totalitarian primacy. This Christianity is a denial and betrayal of the Word that sustains Christian faith itself.

Evangelicals have inherited this disoriented Christianity. The conspiratorial gospel at the heart of this evangelicalism emerged from the pressures of history. It is an inherited gospel that inflames our present time, with great cost.

I'm convinced the way forward involves an honest look backward. It is only by examining the disoriented evangelical inheritance that we can learn how to talk about the living God again. And not just to talk about Godself, but to really encounter the one whose Name is "I will be what I will be." This God is revealed not in acts that fuel paranoia and suspicion, but acts that demonstrate peace and liberation.

A SPECIFIC (AND PERSONAL) PROBLEM

This book looks at how conspiracy theory operates in and in some cases organizes the evangelical movement in America. It contains three related parts. Part one is where we are. Here

I name the pain (and power) associated with conspiracism. Part two is how we got here, in which I trace the history and shape of conspiracy theory in white evangelicalism. And part three is where we need to go, in which I argue for a recovery of *good* suspicion as a survival strategy in a time of Disreality.

Maybe to you, evangelicals are a "they"—a community or abstract demographic with an outsized influence on the political situation. For me, evangelicals have been a "we"—I cannot tell my story without reference to this movement. I have been a son of this house. And I write as someone whose present cannot be explained or narrated without referring back to my time in white evangelicalism. I suppose I can sum it up simply by saying: *If I can change, I believe anyone can.*

That being said, I'm not concerned with repairing what's become of evangelicalism. I agree with Nietzsche: "only where there are graves can there be resurrections"[3]—he was more right than he knew. I'm not writing to rebrand the "evangelical" label, or repair a movement.

In a time of Disreality, my aim is more at the heart of things: a way back to simplicity, humility, and honesty. Not just a return to a set of facts, but a renewal toward a way of living—one open to the possibility of change. And the Christian life, revealed in the story of Jesus, does this very thing.

Maybe you picked up this book and you don't identify as a Christian. Still, you may be a citizen—part of our American society that has been largely influenced by evangelicalism. But at the bedrock, Christian or not, citizen or not, you and I share a humanity in common. Resistance against terrors and tyrannies begins here.

As a practicing Christian, I've gleaned so much from dialogue with atheists, agnostics, and practitioners of other religions. I hope you'll find here compassion for any pain, confusion, and frustration you've endured in the name of Christianity, and perhaps some sense-making of what's at work here in the nexus of conspiracy theory and evangelicalism as a major force today.

You can expect to find open acknowledgment that, yes, evangelicalism has sown immense chaos in America by trampling the weak, robbing the poor, and claiming it all in the name of Jesus. This ongoing catastrophe overflows into the lives of those who have never set foot in an evangelical church.

I believe many who see this Christianity are blameless in asking, "Is *this* what Christian faith is about?" Like William Stringfellow, I, too, have wondered how it happened, how "my people" became the enemy of truth.

Chapter 1

PAIN, PANIC, AND POWER

> When have we ever believed that the world *wasn't* ending?
> What if it always *is* the end of the world?
>
> —Emily St. John Mandel

We live in Disreality.

Conflicting versions of the facts vie for our attention. Families and friendships are divided as entire realities collide, claiming power and wielding incredible force on the world's stage.

We feel Disreality, viscerally. We glimpse it, imperfectly. We breathe it, unknowing. It lurks, unnamed—a steady rising suspicion that much of what we once held in common can no longer be recalled, can no longer be trusted.

In Disreality, we no longer work in common, we no longer

live together. We may *look* at others, but we do not truly *see* one another. Instead, we find ourselves confronted by old tyrannies and new terrors—from the weaponizing of data to new forms of power dressed in academic terms like "network states," "algorithmic warfare," "late fascism," and "techno-feudalism."

We are in desperate need not just of expertise, but wisdom at the level of everyday life.

Disreality—the collision of competing realities—confronts us at every turn. It's an existence felt not just across history, but also in the intimacy of our own lives. It is lived and local. Disreality divides communities and destroys our common world with incredible cost. We are not only divided, we are wrenched apart—our shared reality in ruins.

Disreality is a renaissance of paranoia. One that often comes to us packaged in conspiracy theory. More than the sum total of false facts or half-truths, conspiracy theories are a storytelling act. A single claim spins entire worlds, wielding the power of story, of myth.

These stories wield a power that proves almost impossible to challenge by facts alone. Why? Because they are more myth or story than mere theory. And if conspiracy theories are a storytelling element, they are certainly a radioactive one. The same for disinformation, misinformation, propaganda—all of these elements decay the line between fact and fiction, between truth and falsehood, between what is real and what isn't. Leaving us with the question: What *is* real?

We have lost a grip on common reality in no small part because of how evangelical faith in America has become an agent of Disreality. Supercharged by stories of faith, conspiracy theories come to wield a power greater than alternative facts or convenient fictions. They speak of god and claim the name of Jesus Christ.

Entangled in the Christian story, conspiracy theory becomes the stuff of divine revelation: claiming to expose not just what is "really happening" in the world, what shapes and guides our politics, our societies, and our lives—but *also* who god is. Because of this, conspiracy theory as a story sustained in evangelicalism dangerously malforms Christians with catastrophic consequences for fellow citizens and our common humanity.

Today the question of what Christianity means seems unanswerable. Is it a resource of civilization building? Is it a morality? Is it coercive conquest? The question is mired in the murky waters of conspiracies, political propaganda, and the stories they tell.

In this crisis, the Christian story and its testimony to Jesus is brought under suspicion and called into question. Is Jesus an anti-vaxxer? Does this god call human beings illegal? Does this god sanction camps for "unwanted" populations in the name of "order"?

To "have faith" or claim to be Christian in America isn't settled. It's an unresolved question, an open wound; it is a crisis with consequences for those who claim to be Christian and those who do not. Why? Because we share a world in common. And this world in crisis—a moment of division—calls for decision: Will you, will I, be a person of truth? Can we live in common? Can we provide for one another? Can we pursue justice?

The weight of these questions is sustained and resolved not just by a set of facts and data, but by story. I'm convinced story offers a richer answer to the question "How should we live?" But what happens when the stories that guide and shape us are in need of revision and alteration?

Because of the wild "facts" conspiracy theory peddles, we tend to miss the forest for the trees. Telling the truth is never less than the facts, but always more. In the rush to contend with and dispute spurious facts, we often miss how questionable facts are, together, windows into stories that render reality in a certain way.

Words build worlds.

In Disreality, conspiracy theories are expressions of primal stories at the heart of evangelicalism, of Jesus and America, together. Together, the fusion of these stories expressed by conspiracy theory constructs a functioning reality for millions of American Christians. We are dealing not with reality, but with totality.

Should we be surprised when the stories of conspiracy and Christianity become so entangled that it's impossible to tell one from the other? One person's fact is another's fake news . . . or another's faith. And so questioning these realities initiates a crisis not just of fact, but of faith—revealing the god at the heart of evangelicalism. We find ourselves seemingly trapped in a whole vortex of pain and panic and power, often without the words to define the crisis at its heart.

WHAT IS A CONSPIRACY THEORY?

Identifying conspiracy theories tends to boil down to "you know it when you see it." They immediately strike us with their strange combination of far-fetched facts, anxious suspicion, and secretive overtones. But without a clear definition, we risk confronting conspiracy theories in ways that tend to reinforce our existence in Disreality.

Direct argumentation only causes deeper entrenchment. And dismissing it all as clinical pathology, saying "they're crazy," only divides us further. At the heart of it, we are dealing not just with different fact claims, but also different stories. That makes all the difference.

So let me offer a simple definition that will serve us well: conspiracy theory is a storytelling act that (1) claims what it cannot know and (2) goes beyond what it claims. Conspiracy theory reveals secrets and spins reality.

Take the conspiracy theory that claims we never walked on the moon, for example. The claim itself implies more than a single fact. The claim implies a massive cover-up that metastasizes into a story: NASA is a front, the media is complicit, all of reality is a fraud. These stories always take on this common shape: hidden actors who harbor hostile intent, whose continued existence provokes a sanctified struggle to defeat them.[1]

When we treat conspiracy theory as a storytelling act, we see the crisis raging all around us from a different perspective. We can see that conspiracism within Christian communities isn't a problem to fix with facts, alone. It is a crisis of storytelling, and the consequences of such stories—especially their capacity to cause panic and pain, and seize power—are easily seen across the stream of history.

STORIES THAT PROMOTE PANIC

It was a late fall evening in New Jersey. The date was October 30, 1938, and the United States of America was being invaded. Panic gripped the East Coast. Millions of families huddled around their radios, listening to the unthinkable unfold. An invasion. They were fearing for their lives. Though they didn't need to.

Telephone operators on the clock that night would later recall how their operating boards lit up. Every light a concerned parent, friend, or relative. Someone checking on their family, asking for emergency services, or trying to get updated information from radio stations. All these reactions were caused by one source: a radio program directed by a brash twenty-three-year-old producer by the name of Orson Welles.

That night, though the radio seemed to suggest otherwise, New Jersey wasn't being invaded. Welles was directing a live radio dramatization of the H. G. Wells sci-fi novel *The War of the Worlds*. Welles had pitched it to executives as a live broadcast on radio, a powerful new communication medium, bringing together (and forming) the American consciousness like never before.

Welles's creativity didn't end there. In fact, he decided to push the envelope and present the novel in a particular way, one that invited listeners to experience the story as never before. Welles decided to adapt *The War of the Worlds* as a newscast, a series of news bulletins that basically duplicated the expected format in which most Americans not only consumed daily news, but also received breaking news. It's little surprise, looking back, that the creative format of the radio program supercharged a public panic. The newscasts were so well done, the story so convincing, that they broke the dramatic barrier between fiction and reality. Many Americans listening that night, including those who tuned in late and missed the disclaimer at the beginning of the program, believed the dramatized reports of Martians invading New Jersey. And they acted.

On January 6, 2021, Donald Trump told his supporters gathered on the National Mall in DC that if they didn't "fight like hell" they "weren't going to have a country anymore." The panic was already there. People believed the election was stolen. And that belief had to go somewhere—and fast. Like a volcano, ready to erupt, the mob stormed the Capitol steps. January 6 came and went. Pardons were offered. The same conspiratorial suspicion that fueled the storming of the Capitol now works to sanction a myth that will fuel unrestrained seizures of power and tactics of terror.

Stories that sow panic are powerful political weapons. But they often contain spiritual elements, too. These stories of conspiracy charged by Christian faith stoked a deadly combination of fear and false certainty that has been unleashed on America. January 6 did not happen overnight. The panic was promoted long before.

Back in 1993, evangelist Jerry Falwell started selling a VHS documentary on his popular preaching program, *The Old-Time Gospel Hour*. The documentary wasn't about Jesus, or the church, or theology. It was called *The Clinton Chronicles*, and claimed to expose the corruption of Bill and Hillary Clinton, including baseless claims they were conspiring to murder political opponents. Falwell himself was listed as a producer of the film. And following several special gospel music numbers, and a sermon, Falwell pivoted to peddle this conspiracy theory documentary. But there was little effort to distance the Christian content from the conspiratorial read of current events—in fact, they were presented as one and the same. Falwell told his viewers that "those who know the truth" will be able to discern the facts about the Clintons for themselves. And who are Christians but people who know the truth, right?

The promotion of conspiracy went hand in hand with the feelings of panic that organized the Moral Majority as a new Christian influence on American politics.

For all the ways the alloying of conservatism with evangelicalism manifests itself, and for all the analyses that have been offered to explain this moment, little has been done to examine what happens when theological claims about "truth" are stretched over widespread conspiratorial beliefs, thus including them in a perception called "Christian" or "biblical."

STORIES THAT SEIZE POWER

When looking at Jerry Falwell, perhaps it's little wonder that the Big Lie was so effective among evangelical Christians. For generations, conservative activists and, eventually, Trump allies concentrated in political coalitions and donor networks, like the Council for National Policy, had been sowing doubts, about the left, about Democrats, about the electoral process. These doubts have persisted across American political history, and often have conspiratorial impulses to thank for it.

These doubts seeped in alongside legitimate concerns

like the influence of social media companies or the interference of foreign powers on American elections. But when it came time to mobilize support for the Big Lie leading up to the election of 2020, the propaganda arm of these coalitions, in organizations like Charlie Kirk's Turning Point USA amplified by Salem Radio—the largest conservative Christian radio network in the world—propped up the lie by using overtly theological language, often blaming the "demonic Democrats" and issuing calls to prayer when Trump refused to concede the election.

This demonizing propaganda ensured support for the Big Lie among Christians. By connecting the fact to a more powerful story, it helped keep the claim plausible. The plausibility rested not in the *facts* of the case, but in their association with the authority reflected in the Christian story.

Taken this way, it didn't matter whether Democrats actually stole an election. What mattered, and what any "biblical" Christian knows, is that Democrats are the kind of people *who would* steal an election—or so the story goes. The theological and moral plausibility of the Big Lie justified the violence to come.

It's one thing to engineer panic. It's another to exploit it, to direct it, to harness it for a particular purpose. And evangelical Christianity is bound up in this problem. As one Capitol Police officer later testified to Congress, "It was clear the terrorists perceived themselves to be Christians."[2] Everything depends on the stories we tell.

STORIES THAT CAUSE PAIN AND LEAVE SCARS

A study by Sophia Moskalenko found something startling, but not surprising. "Participants with a QAnon loved one reported higher anxiety and PTSD than those without such connection"—those affected by conspiracy theories endure significant levels of mental and emotional stress and even trauma.[3] The burden of conspiracy theory is felt not just in a rational or political sense, but spans the emotional and relational register, too.

I was raised in a fundamentalist stream of evangelicalism, so I know this firsthand. We were hard-liners: critical of Billy Graham for his relationships with Catholics, the "wrong kind of Christian" according to fundamentalist evangelicals. Anxiety came with the territory. It often manifested in conspiratorial narrations about all that was different or unknown.

Decades later as a pastor, I heard church members share they believed Tom Hanks was a closet pedophile, that the 2020 election was stolen, and that QAnon's prophecies of a coming storm to sweep away corrupt elites would be realized in Trump. Right alongside the conspiracy theory was Christian confession, and there was little difference offered between one and the other.

My pastoral introduction to QAnon came in the middle of protests against racism and police brutality. I watched people I love post the #SaveTheKids hashtag (a gateway to QAnon) as the comeback to #BlackLivesMatter. The potential for dialogue was destroyed by the speed of conspiratorial storytelling. The story of stolen children, as always a mixture of fact and fiction,[4] gave the moral high ground back to those who wanted to silence talk of race and police brutality in America.

I'd be willing to bet most of you reading this have developed an idea or two about why people buy conspiracy theories like these. Pain has forced many of us to seek answers for the loss and the loneliness. Conspiracism isn't an academic problem to be solved in order to "fix people." It isn't a disease that demands clinical intervention. It's an act of storytelling that attempts to express the inexpressible, to channel fear into certainty, to narrate the complex by rendering it simple. This appeals to friends, family, and coworkers—if we're honest, because we are human: it appeals to all of us at some level. The scale of the problem is matched only by the force of the crisis felt in our closest, most intimate relationships.

Maybe you have felt at a loss. Not only over why someone might believe these things. But also navigating the "living loss" of relationships, of influence and intimacy. This is why I'm slow to offer immediate corrections to our self-made reflections on conspiracy theory. Because I've found these ideas are incubated in times of suffering, loss, and confusion.

And in these moments of loss, we grasp at all sorts of

explanations: "They're afraid. They're angry. They're anxious. They're crazy." Elements of these explanations might contain a kernel of truth. But they don't paint the whole picture. And this is where the risk comes in.

Because as soon as we conclude, for example, that our friend, our coworker is "crazy," well—that might allow us not only to dismiss them, but also dehumanize them. No one likes being disillusioned. But much of how we try to argue against conspiracy theory tends to ignore this basic nature of human existence. People turn to conspiracism to express a variety of things.

It helps to recognize how recent scholarship distinguishes between conspiracy theory and the act of conspiracy *theorizing*. The storytelling act of conspiracy theory offers "community and power to people who feel—or are—marginalized in society, particularly in the digital realm."[5] But, as ever, the stories we tell construct worlds of either healing or harm. This is why so much depends on the stories we tell and the tapestry of truth they contain.

FROM PAIN TO PARANOIA

This combination of pain, panic, and power that I've previewed here is a window into a dangerous paranoia at work among Christians in America. So the question is: "Are you calling Christians crazy?" Yes and no.

As a practicing Christian, I admit: there's an unavoidable scandal at the heart of Christian faith. It is a faith that confesses God became man in a first-century Jew whose life as an itinerant rabbi resulted in his crucifixion as an insurrectionist by Roman occupiers. This man, Jesus, did not stay dead. Christian faith confesses this Jesus was resurrected and so vindicated by God as humanity's deliverance from sin, evil, and death.

Confessing Christians will readily concede this scandal. But it does not follow that this confession necessarily issues in rampant, raging conspiracism—the kind organizing our society and our politics. Nevertheless, this is just what has happened. The stories of conspiracism have become indistinguishable from a certain way of being Christian in America.

And as this Christianity attempts to narrate the world around itself, it makes use of conspiracy theory to give its gospel urgency, relevancy, and even moral power. Raging conspiracism has indeed been at the heart of evangelicalism from the very beginning. We will see this in the pages to come.

This raging conspiracism illustrates one of the central arguments of this book: conspiracy theories are doing theological work for the evangelicals who believe them. This isn't to discount other dimensions of conspiracy theory.

Psychology can tell us how conspiracy theories seize on our cognitive biases, how they satisfy our need for belonging or identity and meaning. Information science can tell us how conspiracy theories assemble information, and they can criticize the quality and sources of such information. Political science and security studies can tell us about the role conspiracy theories play in political parties and their hand in radicalization. We need more seats at the table, not fewer.

But whenever and however conspiracy theories entangle themselves with the story of Christian faith, we have to recognize theology as both problem and solution.

Distorting the Christian story beyond recognition calls for the renewal and rightsizing of what was always meant to be a good-news story. We will see this in greater detail in a future chapter. My aim here is to name the crisis of evangelical conspiracy, defined by something I call "holy paranoia."

Some will read "holy paranoia" and dismiss it as a slogan. A cover for another "baseless" attack on otherwise "biblical" people who are not just misunderstood but also persecuted.

Others hear "holy paranoia" and see something familiar, a name for your lived experience. Holy paranoia encapsulates how relationships and communities have fractured or been seemingly destroyed by a conspiracism supercharged by faith, a vision of Jesus whose announcing of the kingdom of God is one and the same with MAGA authoritarianism.

What do I mean by "holy paranoia"? To put "holy" together with "paranoia" is my way of naming the problem at the heart of this conspiratorial gospel. "Holy" in the most basic sense has always referred to a sense of "otherness." The otherness I have in mind here is the unique but potent dimension of conspiracism supercharged by Christian faith.

And paranoia? This *isn't* pathological. It's "splitness" or fracture at the very center of Christ himself. Holy paranoia names how American evangelicals inherit a split portrait of Jesus. This is a Jesus at odds with himself. A Jesus so committed to American might that America's enemies are *his* enemies.

This contradictory Christ, this conspiratorial gospel, spins dangerous stories of devotion. Believing in this paranoiac Jesus, those who take the name Christian are primed to receive certain conspiracy theories as not just *plausible* in the realm of facts. It's deeper than that. It's a plausibility that is equated with faith, with what is perceived and received as *biblical*.

Holy paranoia is a crisis of disoriented faith. And it's a crisis in many dimensions. Across its history, evangelicals in America have always been suspicious of those at the bottom of the social order, on the margins, or those who deviate from that order. Conspiracies emerge as a live exercise in trying to maintain this hold on order and certainty, and tend to cast those at the bottom, on the borders, or those deemed "bad" as the threat. This is why disproving one conspiracy theory fails to get at the heart of it all. It's not just a single narrative, but a perception of how the world works, and who God is.

I hope naming this perception liberates us from unhelpful caricatures that persist in our moment. Referring to someone as "paranoid" tends to invoke clinical language, specifically pathologies and medical treatments. We need to hold space for clinical conditions where paranoid visions feature as symptoms. We should not rush to pathologize. I want to caution against that very thing here. I'm not trying to give a medical diagnosis.

Instead, by putting these words together—"Holy paranoia"—I'm inviting reflection on a unique problem: theological split-mindedness, a Jesus who is defined as much by fear, suspicion, and rage as he is by faith, hope, and love.

Holy paranoia names this deeper crisis of faith in a Christianity trying to point to the story of Christ while sustaining myths of American greatness and whiteness. These two stories have become so deeply entangled that they construct a totality, a lens for interpreting reality that again seeks to speak for the whole. This totality is a theological corruption. Current "best practices" of disinformation activism cannot touch this distinctly Christian problem.

Disreality reveals those who have received the Christian story, and those who have seized it, shattering the whole. Now, the shards of this story are used to sanction authoritarianism. But there was a time when these shards were wielded with great effect. Some of us have the scars to show for it.

HOLY PARANOIA AND ME

The Irish novelist James Joyce recognized that the particular contained the universal.[6] The more I've spoken of my own experience in evangelical Christianity in America, the more I'm confronted with a contradiction: some say, "Me too!" while others shout, "How dare you!"

When I announced I was writing this book, a friend from a church I went to as a college student reached out. She's now a clinical psychologist. What she said stuck with me: "So many of my clients are having difficulty untangling the conspiratorial stuff from their faith." My experience, your experience—these aren't isolated incidents. Since 2021, white evangelicals have consistently polled as one of the religious groups with the highest affinity for the tenets of QAnon at nearly one in four, or 25 percent.[7] The emergence and mainstreaming of QAnon into our zeitgeist could not have happened without evangelicalism.

Conspiracy theory isn't a bug, but a feature of evangelical Christianity in America. Conspiracy theory—because it is so prominent in American culture—always has a ready reception in American evangelicalism. And the ascendancy of conspiracism in our social and political moment has included evangelicals along with it. First, conspiracy theory traversed evangelical media networks like Moody and

Christianity Today; now it is supercharged by evangelical activists, like the late Charlie Kirk and Sean Feucht.

And yet, I'm comfortable recognizing that the experiences emerging out of evangelicalism are diverse and varied, too. Like a nesting doll, there are subcultures inside of the whole. Especially beyond the United States. There are Palestinian evangelicals. There are Sudanese evangelicals.

We tend to miss this because, at least in terms of American partisan politics, evangelicalism tends to be understood as one big thing: a voting bloc with patterned and predictable ideological commitments and partisan loyalty.

But in an existential sense, evangelicalism is a living, evolving thing. It has its broad fronts of fundamentalism, closets of silenced LGBTQ+ Christians, segregated ethnic minorities, and cloisters of elite oligarchs. Being "evangelical" is always contested.

Evangelicalism is a labyrinth, not a monolith. And over the last decade, especially with histories like *Jesus and John Wayne* or *The Other Evangelicals*, there are new stories being told of particular pockets and networks that are proving resonant universally *because* they home in on something particular. Conspiracy theory is no different.

And so when I tell my story, I do so not because I believe it's a universal account, but rather my own particular commitment to tell the truth about what I've seen and heard, what has shaped me and continues to do so; it is in this smallness that resonance with the experiences of others is born.

FUNDAMENTALISM

I was raised in a fundamentalist offshoot of evangelical Christianity. This meant that there was still revival preaching and talk of being "born again." But with an added element of zealous purity. For example, we used the King James Version of the Bible, insisting that it was the only version approved by God. Those who didn't were subjected to a mixture of communal disapproval that prefigured the dread they should feel awaiting God's judgment.

At my childhood church, the fault line between "evangelical" and "fundamentalist" grew more apparent as I got older. There were those in our church who might call Jerry Falwell or Billy Graham liberal for their politics, for reaching across the ecclesial divide to build political coalitions with charismatics and Catholics.

But there were also those who shrugged their shoulders. Over the years, as I've gone back and had conversations with parents, people who were my Sunday School teachers, I realized two things. First, many have changed—they either no longer attend church or attend nondenominational churches. A few recalled their own ways of resisting the fundamentalist extremes of the church at the time, like expressing doubts over certain decisions. That change is significant, I think. But the problem of conspiracism persists.

I grew up hearing a gospel that was constantly framed by conspiratorial suspicions. And for outsiders, I want to emphasize just how entangled this was. There was no discrimination between conspiracy theory or "alternative facts" and the Christian story. They were one and the same. As a kid, I rarely heard any critical distinctions offered between critiques of Bill Clinton and the Democrats and the preaching of salvation: you were either on the right side, or you weren't.

If a preacher made a passing comment about the rise of a one-world government, it was taken as "biblical" truth. Coming to Jesus was synonymous with distrust in government, suspicion over new technologies like barcodes or payment systems, and anxieties over coming persecution of Christians. These all converged together in—and were supercharged by—theology. To question one is to create a crisis for all of it.

Growing up, those who claimed a "biblical worldview" were not talking merely about theology, but about a whole set of claims emerging *from* Christian confession out into economics, to politics, to science. For example, "biblical worldview" talk curated suspicion over scientific expertise. We had a whole slew of visiting speakers who routinely shared archeological or biological "evidence" that apparently contradicted the consensus of scientists.

I remember one speaker vividly. For a kid who watched Indiana Jones growing up, the idea of a biblical archeologist coming to speak was electric. His name was Ron Wyatt. In his videos, he claimed to have discovered Noah's ark, submerged Egyptian chariots at the bottom of the Red Sea (the remnants of forces sent after Moses in the Exodus), and—of course—the Ark of the Covenant.

Ron Wyatt's work has been broadly discredited, from historians to archeologists. He was, by his credentials, not an archeologist but a nurse anesthetist. But in the circles I grew up in, lack of credentials from so-called secular sources was a *credit* to his claims. Being a self-appointed expert who told a story of being ostracized from various academic guilds was a credential in and of itself.

And so, I *believed* this, too. It gave credibility to the wider story I was being taught. Noah's ark, the Ark of the Covenant, all of it "factual," gave me confidence that my faith was *true* and *real*. It was a confidence I even expressed, when I argued with a Bible teacher at my Christian school, insisting that *yes*, the Ark of the Covenant had been found. "They shared it at my church last night!" I said out loud in class. Words from the pulpit were, in my mind, the necessary proof of its validity and credibility. That's the innocence of children, and the responsibility of adults.

There wasn't just suspicion of history and archeology. There was partisan suspicion, too, over all things Democrat or "liberal"—a charge with such power that you didn't even need to define your terms. It was common to hear these buzzwords laced into preaching. I didn't know much of what they meant, only what their existence *meant for me*. "The liberals" were godless, coming for Christians like us, and it would all get much worse before the return of Christ.

There was an "us" and a "them" that—upon greater reflection—seems to correspond so nicely to the "saved" and "damned" identities that I believed were at the heart of any and all difference. This is the uncritical power of conspiracy, too.

MARTYR MYTHS

The constant suspicion from every direction gave rise to a persecution complex. I suppose it has always been there. Evangelicals in America have long nursed the belief that we are a persecuted minority while wielding majority power. Central to this paradox are the myths of martyrdom that reinforce it. Take the assassination of Charlie Kirk. A tragic act of political violence perpetrated by digital nihilism was absorbed by a potent and primal story: that Kirk died as an exemplar of Christian faith. Holy paranoia gave meaning to a tragic act of political violence: he was not just murdered, so the story goes, he was a martyr. His frequent casting of aspersions on non-white Americans with the Great Replacement conspiracy theory or promoting the Big Lie of election fraud in 2020 as a matter of faithful Christianity. As always, the stories that sustain evangelicalism give rise to convenient forgettings and fictions in the name of what is biblical. Kirk's martyrdom was not the first time this persecution complex performed its task.

I was nine years old when the Columbine school shooting shocked America. Being a kid, I didn't really watch the news. But the shooting at Columbine High School in Colorado affected me and a generation of evangelical youth groups because of how it curated devotion by propagating the myth of evangelical persecution.

In the wake of the shooting, the memory of Columbine generated this ethos of radical faith bound up in martyrdom. It was, I think, the sum of grief and shock, mixed with an anxiety over cultural collapse and a persecution complex *that already existed*. In the wake of Columbine, this entire ethos of persecution and martyrdom permeated my years in youth group. It was an ethos that would give zeal to my faith, and define the ideal of what a commitment to Jesus should look like.

This ethos came to rely on the story of Cassie Bernall, a student who was tragically shot and killed after allegedly answering "yes" when asked at gunpoint whether she believed in God by one of the shooters.

Michael W. Smith, one of the most famous and prolific Christian artists in the contemporary Christian music industry, wrote a song about her. Her story was published in a book written a mere five months after her murder. It was authored by her parents. The book was titled *She Said Yes*, and its story became the prototype faith that fueled my years in youth group.

Countless sermons—from youth all-nighters to devotions to Wednesday night rallies—ended with Cassie's story as the climax. This had the effect of giving me the impression that *this* exchange, between a teenage executioner asking his classmates about their faith, was the *sole* question I had to prepare for. The Columbine martyrs became the prototype for radical faith that I was supposed to have, that my own faith was measured by.

I guess it's little wonder I struggled with doubt, over whether I was really a Christian. Because the ethos that framed my faith—its intensity and authenticity—was an ethos that suggested you could never really know if you had faith unless you were staring down the barrel of a gun. I can't put a number on how many times I thought about what I'd do if I was forced to identify as a Christian at gunpoint.

But Cassie Bernall was never asked if she believed in God. She never said yes. In a tragic case of mistaken identity, quite literally the fog of war, a student misreported the actual student who said yes, Valeen Schnurr, as Cassie. Valeen survived. This case of mistaken identity is understandable. The fog of war, the shroud of grief, all of it contributed to a wild misunderstanding about what had happened in the library at Columbine High School.

What is less justifiable is how the evangelical world pressed on with the martyrdom narrative and ethos. I was able to find two separate articles published in *The Denver Post* that recount the accurate version of events within months of *She Said Yes* hitting the bookshelves.[8] First, an article published within a week of the shooting itself recounts Valeen's return home from the hospital and her recollections of her exchange with the shooters on her faith. Another article, published in September of 1999, the same month as *She Said Yes* was released, reports on the conflicting account of Emily Wyant, who was hiding with Cassie under the table. In the article, Emily contradicts the narrative of the book *She Said Yes*—sharing that, as they hid under the table together, Cassie was never spoken to before she was shot.

Let's not lose sight of the human element. I know from my work as a hospice chaplain that grief always seeks meaning and purpose. I'm sure that, for Cassie's parents, the idea of such a clear account that seemed to confirm what they believed had been true of their daughter—a kind, courageous, faithful human—was compelling.

When, in the weeks that followed, differing accounts emerged, it must have been incredibly difficult for survivors and their parents, for all who never got to say goodbye, to reconsider and rework the narratives that had settled in their neurological systems as survival strategies, stories to cope with the tragedy. Conspiracy theorizing is similar in this respect. We can and must create space for human limits and frailty when it comes to the truth.

Leaving this space for acknowledgment frees those of us who were on the receiving end of the ethos of martyrdom that took root in American evangelicalism in the wake of Columbine. This ethos evolved and expanded, but it was given life by a single solitary commitment: do not let facts get in the way of a good story. The idea of a martyred teenager was, in the end, too compelling for an evangelical culture not only looking for content to narrate its time but also trying to find its footing so as to deliver its gospel with urgency and relevancy.

The evangelical reception of Columbine was a harbinger of the holy paranoia that we contend with today. Writing for *Vox*, Alissa Wilkinson traced some of the martyrdom myths of Columbine and the "cottage industry" that emerged in the American church to capitalize on the story. But she, too, recognizes the human element:

> Most of the people who rushed to tell the stories of Bernall and Scott after the horrific events of Columbine did so with good intentions: to grieve, to commemorate loss, and to inspire courage in teenagers who were reeling from sudden instability and fear. But in a now-familiar pattern, their stories were turned into banners for causes, mythologies that couldn't be altered by the truth. They were fed into

a wider narrative that continues to profoundly affect American public culture at large.[9]

There's a thread of holy paranoia in these words: "Stories were turned into banners for causes, mythologies that couldn't be altered by the truth." Theses myths of Columbine emerged from a place of deep grief, yes. The same can be said of Kirk, and the brutal tragedy of political violence. But there are those who exploited them, propagated them, in youth groups and on radio shows across America, to give the rising generation a "radical" faith based less on truth and more on perception, on suspicion, on what resonated and *worked*.

For *my* evangelicalism, Columbine became a site of tragedy and exploitation, the kind that propagated a version of events that confirmed what evangelicals *suspected* was true of the world around them. And they told stories to that effect.

NARRATING THE END OF THE WORLD

In her brilliant book *Coming of Age in the War on Terror*, Randa Abdel-Fattah writes, "Suspicion doesn't create an actual community. It creates an imagined one."[10]

I remember a missionary returning from the UK in the months just after September 11. I was eleven years old. And on a Sunday night, I listened to a sermon that, very much like Billy Graham's Cold War sermons against communism, warned our church that unless Americans repented, we'd be overrun by Muslims—something that he claimed was already happening in the UK, where he lived. I remember that sermon all these years later. I suppose the reason I do is because my church told me missionaries were people who loved the people they lived with in countries not my own.

Fear of "the other" is sustained by stories, not just bad facts. Camps are built and people are disappeared downriver of stories that sustain a culture and sanction its fears. Donald Trump seized on these fears to activate his first candidacy for president through casting suspicion on President Obama's citizenship.

It mattered little whether it was *true*. What mattered was that such a narrative, such a story, aligned with what many had come to suspect was adjacent to the Christian story they believed: that Jesus was their Lord and that Obama was, among other things, anti-Christian, anti-American, and liberal.

Sometimes it doesn't matter if conspiracy theories are true or not. What matters is that they give voice to vibes, to put it simply. The sense that Obama was not good for Christians overwhelmed any and all factually grounded considerations about his citizenship. The fact that he was Black, that his name was not Anglo-Saxon, all of this converged and combined to give the Birther conspiracy lasting influence. It was, perhaps, the earliest organizing story of the community that came to be known as MAGA.

CONSPIRACIES AND PASTORING

When I decided to go to Jerry Falwell's Liberty University for college, people in my church expressed concern. The concern was I'd become a liberal. It's true. That's the sort of evangelical fundamentalism I grew up in. Not as embittered as Westboro Baptist picketing the funerals of veterans, but suspicious of Billy Graham and Jerry Falwell because they politically organized with Catholics, who were endlessly suspect within fundamentalist evangelicalism for not being the right kind of Christian.

For me, Liberty was a step *out* into a broader world of evangelical, conservative coalitions. A shocker, I know. But while in Lynchburg, the idea of a "Christian nation" continued to be reinforced and remained obvious to me. There was nothing that I encountered in these spaces that was much different from what I had always known. I passed a class called Creation Studies that taught six-day creation against evolution. I fasted for a John McCain victory during the presidential race of 2008. I remember not understanding the elation expressed by some students when Obama won. The significance of his election in and among the

African American experience was unintelligible to me, rendered so by the spaces that shaped my childhood, which of course were overwhelmingly white. I had no language for white supremacy, no way to articulate racism beyond personal animosity into dimensions of collective erasure and systemic terror.

The stubborn persistence of conspiracy theory—something that had always lain dormant in my evangelical experience—began to *matter* more acutely in the first term of Trump's presidency. In years that saw a national reckoning over police brutality and racism, from the Charlottesville rally in 2017 to the demonstrations and revolutionary violence of 2020, together with the COVID-19 pandemic, the conspiratorial heartbeat of evangelical Christianity was exposed in a way that was *not* surprising, but still shocking.

I was a college pastor in Fredericksburg, Virginia, during the first lockdown of COVID. I remember the moment when I knew conspiracy theory was emerging with a new potency. In those first few chaotic weeks, when we didn't know much of anything beyond our anxious need to be prepared, I purchased two small digital thermometers for our ministry. It was a cautious, preparatory move. I didn't know where it was all heading, or what was about to happen. I figured these things might be hard to get a hold of in the next couple weeks, and purchased them with no plan of how or if I would use them. Then, word got out.

Word got back to me that a parent was deeply opposed to

the "fact" that I was going to be using these thermometers to keep people out of church, that I was denying people's civil liberties, that he'd keep his kids from coming—the list of accusations went on, all tied to what the *liberals* were trying to do behind the scenes of the COVID response. This rumor-mongering was a shot across the bow. A warning. It woke me up. The pandemic was weeks old. Knowledge was scarce. But somehow, the people I served already had the answers. Had already taken a stand and a position.

This pandemic was itself a small apocalypse. It revealed a totalizing theological ideology *already* present in the evangelical mind. This totality was inherited, and associated with being "biblical." I didn't have the words then for the contradiction. But I've since recognized the danger: if what you are is "biblical," then you can never consider how you might be wrong.

I've since understood this as the sort of knowledge holy paranoia excels at producing, where bits of ideology and conspiracy and primal story are packaged up and presented as unchallengeable Christian faith. I was not prepared to consider this totality in its entirety. I had no way of naming this corruption; I inherited the very certainty that fused other stories with the story of Jesus. I thought I could repair it apart from having my own faith turned upside down. I was wrong.

Outsiders tend to assume that Christian nationalism or evangelical conspiracism spreads through explicit preaching and things like that. And it does, but it spreads through coded silence or tacit slogans that betray deeper ideological roots in primal myths and stories. The simple truth is that a great number of evangelical churches have—for generations—served the bread and wine of Christ from a party platform. The party line is not the boundary of Christian communion. But conspiracy theory often holds that line. This cannot be repaired; it demands repentance—that Christian word for a death that comes before resurrection.

PEOPLE WHO KNOW THE TRUTH

There was an ancient sect of Christianity that claimed salvation was akin to knowing. It was liberation not from death and evil but from bodily existence itself, and the path was laid by traversing paths of secret knowledge. They were called "gnostics" or "knowers" by the Church Father Irenaeus. They understood salvation to be less to do with the broken, crucified, and risen body of Jesus and more to do with accessing hidden knowledge. Salvation for the gnostics was a path that promised escape from the world, and it was a path paved by secrets. This isn't that much different from the way conspiracy theory flows through the evangelical mind.

"People who know the truth," that's how the evangelical pastor and political activist Jerry Falwell defended the credibility of the conspiratorial documentary he produced on the

Clintons in the early 90s and sold on his television preaching ministry.[11] I met him as a high school student. "Truth" as I experienced it inside evangelicalism wasn't just the truth of Christ, but that truth stretched over and applied to all sorts of incredible, conspiratorial claims.

What happens when those who claim to *know*, don't? Then as now, Irenaeus understood that sometimes such falsehood appears "more true than the truth itself."[12] This conspiratorial gospel diverges from the Christian story and the Word of the crucified. And what makes it so pernicious is that it claims to possess what is "biblical" or "Christian," which also makes it dangerous—because falsehood always defends itself by violence.

We are faced with this crisis of Disreality in several dimensions; at the heart of the crisis for evangelicalism and the influence it wields in America is a conspiratorial gospel. It lies at the heart of evangelical Christianity in America, the product of stories about God and country and culture that form its totality and identity. It's a totality that cannot be questioned, an identity forged by myths and stories with a history; and it is a story that we have so often failed to tell. One reason for that failure is our focus on facts, not just the stories themselves.

Chapter 2

POWER OF STORY

> We are, I guess, all of us, built out of stories.
>
> —James Rebanks

As novelist Rebecca West recalled the unpredictable series of events that sparked World War I over a century ago, she admitted, "'I shall never be able to understand how it happened.' It is not that there are too few facts available, but that there are too many."[1]

Speaking for her generation, West prophetically described ours. We are awash in facts and data. And it's the irony of our time that in spite of the mass of facts and data, we are experiencing a near total fracture of trust in a shared reality. How did we get here?

In 1981, Richard Buckminster introduced what he called the "knowledge doubling curve" concept.[2] He estimated that humanity's repository of information by 1900 had roughly doubled every century. By the end of World War II, Buckminster estimated humanity's information doubled every twenty-five years. Now, present estimates range from a year to twelve hours. It's little wonder that Disreality is the norm.

Disreality is a state of existence defined by a desire for both meaning *and* certainty—almost at any cost. This desire primes people for the authoritarian playbook, and leaders who seem to create their own reality. Often under the guise of "telling it like it is," authoritarians are, above all, storytellers, the sustainers of myths of the nation. The state of Disreality is the soil for authoritarians and totalitarianism.

But Disreality in our time isn't about a lack of fact, but an overload. Disreality is a default on common reality. The information revolution gives us more facts than we know what to do with. It's a revolution of size *and* speed. All our interconnected devices (from smart watches to refrigerators to coffeepots), sometimes collectively referred to as the "internet of things," capture mass quantities of consumer data—not just browsing history, but behaviors, habits, *anything useful* to developers and profiteers.

When we combine the internet of things with the explosion of generative and analytical AI, we have to reckon with the mass scale of information and the breakneck speed of duplication. Conspiracy theories thrive in this environment.

Think of information like a river. Every molecule of water a parcel of fact or data. But then, imagine factories lining the riverbanks. These represent media corporations, marketing firms, partisan think tanks, politicians and their lackeys. Each dumping toxic sludge into the stream, a combination of false facts, propaganda, disinformation, muddies the water even more.

Now, what happens when this information river overflows its banks? When the toxic stream becomes a torrential flood with dangerous rapids? Suddenly, facts alone aren't enough. But we struggle to see this because modernity tells us facts are all we have.

PRIMAL STORIES AND FACT

The word "fact" comes to us via Latin, *factum*. It originally meant "an event," or "a happening." We might describe a fact as simply "what is." But in our moment, fact has been stretched past the breaking point to "what is *unquestionable*." To the authoritarian, the State is a fact. To the capitalist, the free market is a fact. Labeling something a "fact" today signifies not just an event, but something that cannot be questioned or protested.

We've moved beyond fact as a common event and into a perilous state of Disreality where what is fact signifies the exercise of raw power. Facts are created in Disreality seemingly out of thin air.

In his classic study of propaganda, sociologist Jacques Ellul argues the "fact" becomes an object of worship. Ellul wrote, "The fact dictates the things that are and so cannot be questioned. Modern man worships 'facts'—that is, he accepts 'facts' as the ultimate reality. He is convinced that what is, is good. He believes that facts in themselves provide evidence and proof, and he willingly subordinates values to them; he obeys what he believes to be necessity."[3]

Ellul's analysis can be seen all around us, even in the stories we tell about our time. In the film *Don't Look Up*, humanity is threatened by an asteroid careening toward Earth. The impact will cause a mass extinction event—billions will die. That is the event confronting humanity. But in the film, the president of the United States, played by actor Meryl Streep, uses a reelection campaign slogan as a fact of raw power: "Don't look up!"

This slogan became a "fact"—created by raw power—organizing the lives of those whose totality refused to accommodate the reality of impending catastrophe. Discriminating the difference between fact as "that which is" versus "that which cannot be questioned" helps us name how denial or domination or greed can become a "fact" in totalities that tempt us to accept these things as "the way things are."

To put it simply, just by saying something "is" doesn't make it fact. My aim here isn't to promote distrust in facts, but rather pinpoint how dressing *everything* as a fact through dictatorial power erodes our capacity to parse fact from fiction.

This is totalitarianism. Historian and philosopher Hannah Arendt recognized it as such when she observed, "The ideal subject of totalitarian rule is not the convinced Nazi or the convinced Communist, but people for whom the distinction between fact and fiction (i.e., the reality of experience) and the distinction between true and false (i.e., the standards of thought) no longer exist."[4]

We have failed to realize that an overreliance on "fact" to give us a workable reality for political action has primed us for totalitarianism. This is because totalities tend to invite us to perceive the movers and shakers of the world as "fact"—nation-states, economic systems, political leaders—merely because we cannot imagine a world without them.

Without realizing it, we've cast forces and systems that shape our world as "facts" simply because we assume their givenness. We hold facts and data as the raw (but also the most reliable) material from which we construct our own existence and tell our own stories. Just facts, we say, are enough. There's a danger here.

TOTALITY, NOT REALITY

Journalist Charlie Warzel, writing for *The Atlantic*, argues we are enduring "a cultural assault on any person or institution that operates in reality."[5] He's put his finger on the pulse of Disreality and its polarizing persecution of expertise and knowledge.

And this is good, because I'm convinced we need better language to name this problem.

I'm not disputing or discrediting the need for evidence and hard fact. What I'm suggesting is that we are missing the way story sorts and selects which facts appear as plausible or possible to us. These stories, operating at a primal level, converge to construct a condition or state I call "totality."

Totality is the *experience* of reality as a bounded whole, and as such, it presents as a single view and vantage that postures to speak for *all* reality. There's not one, but many. Totalities are constructed by stories that store, sort, and interpret facts. They make some things appear "obvious" or "right" while others "spurious" and "wrong." And the point is, we all tend toward totalities. We inhabit them like a home; we consume them like the air we breathe.

Again, I'm not here to offer a tacit endorsement to the raging, dangerous trend of anti-science or anti-intellectualism. I'm here to nudge us to consider the limits of facts and data when it comes to naming and experiencing what we call "reality." And in Disreality, there are many totalities on offer.

Facts and data are merely raw bits of information that give us insight into what philosopher Giorgio Agamben calls "bare" life.[6] Bare life is like your vital signs, but I am talking about your life story. These are not mutually exclusive.

In my vocation as a hospice chaplain, I can read a patient's chart and see their vitals, but I know better than to assume that someone's life and existence can be contained to the facts of their chart. I always ask about their story. It doesn't dispute the facts of their diagnosis, but it does illuminate what has determined them beyond that diagnosis to make them who they are.

In the same way, we might scale Agamben's idea of "bare" life to "bare" reality, a world constructed by the sum total of raw fact and data. Who (or what) gives meaning to that world? Science is suited for bare reality. Its knowledge is helpful and useful. But reality is more than what is bare and void. Bare reality is the bedrock from which facts are mined and extracted. But it is story that refines facts and invests them with meaning, both individually and collectively.

Story, not facts, offers an answer to the question "How should we live?" It's a question we all ask (and live) implicitly. It's not a question confined to introductory ethics courses in school. It's a question contained in and answered by story.

We need story. Fact alone cannot carry forward the meaning or interpretation of a "happening." And yet, all of us live in a world dominated by the prevailing assumption that "reality" and "the data" are synonymous. What we mean, really, is that "bare reality" and data are synonymous.

Few historians will discredit the fact that a man named Jesus of Nazareth was crucified by the Romans. But all these facts are still devoid of meaning apart from the refining of story. The meaning of this crucifixion? The scandalous, incredible claim of resurrection? There is always story interpreting and assigning meaning. We are always living answers to that question, how should we live? And story gives us the imagination to act.

At the height of the racial protests in 2020, I remember a conversation with a church member where, no matter how much I shared factual economic disparities, there were no common shared "facts" that would unseat his suspicion that white and Black Americans were not divided by anything more than laziness. Beneath the racism was a story that organized his world. It led him to understand poverty as a moral failing rooted in (and perpetuated by) a racist understanding of cultural elitism and supremacy. Because of this racist dimension of his totality and the stories that upheld it, facts proved insufficient in altering the totalizing reality reflected in his perception. But the story was the seed from which everything emerged.

There are facts that, ultimately, make no difference in convincing someone. Armed with facts but helpless to argue someone to our point of view leaves us feeling at a loss for how to forge any sort of common political will toward solving common problems.

Polarization is the disfunction conspiracism wreaks in a society. But it is also the damage it causes in more intimate spaces. All of this has us reaching for some sort of objective standard, some sort of shared sense of commonality by which to judge the viability and veracity of specific claims. And there's much to be said for this. But I want to point out the limits of this approach.

The version of reality rendered by "the data" isn't comprehensive. We could lay out every "fact" about ourselves—from eye color and favorite movies to Social Security number and tax bracket—and we will still not capture the essence of who we are; we will not be seen as complex and concrete human beings.

The limits of data are important to recall in a time when so many facts and data are contested and conflicting in a state of Disreality. Conspiracy theory operates at this higher plane of "full reality"—it offers an account of an event or even an entire moment in history as myth. As Jeff Sharlet observes when it comes to fascism, "You cannot fact check a myth."[7]

So where does this leave us? I want to suggest that a different set of questions renders the problem of conspiracism baked into Christianity in a new light. How does conspiracism express the theology and ideology that binds evangelicalism? How does is operate as a mode of storytelling or mythmaking beyond "bare reality" to promote a particularly Christian and American totality?

Through the myths and stories it tells about America and Christ, this totality comes to not just shape perception, but create it. To tell this story is to offer an answer for how we should live that issues to perilous threats to any and all coded as enemies or heretics or partisan opposites.

We've all heard the slogan "perception is reality"—well, that is what totality offers. Perception renders that which becomes real to us. And that reality, this totality, holds us captive.

The great Roman orator Cicero coined this term "perception." And perhaps we need to talk about it again from the very roots. Taken from the Latin *percipio*, the concept of perception refers not just to *what* we see but *how*. The Roman poet Ovid used *percipio* (which literally means "through seizure") to talk about understanding. Perception refers to our cognitive ability to gather and interpret information.

Totality goes beyond bare life, and takes up raw information to invest it with meaning. Here, human perception goes to work. It gathers, it assigns, it weighs—it interprets. We can see here how there are really no limits to how many totalities can exist.

For evangelicals, the idea of a "biblical worldview" often signals their operative totality. But totalities can arise anywhere and everywhere, in fandom communities focused on *Star Wars*, in lifestyle movements focused on diets or exercise, in partisan movements. Totality names the experience of enclosure, that sense of unity and certainty afforded by a single, shared perspective.

Naming totality and the way it curates perception gives us the language to begin to articulate how a movement like evangelical Christianity, one that claims to stand for "objective truth" in all its forms, has become an agent of Disreality. It wields its totality in a mode of domination *and* distortion with incredible cost.

THE TOTALITY OF A BIBLICAL WORLDVIEW

It will be helpful here to make a specific illustration of this cost. Totality cultivates perception, and perception frames plausibility and possibility. Beyond the borders of totality, then, is everything lost to those who inhabit it. This is true for each and every one of us. But when it comes to evangelicalism, the cost of this loss reveals the distortion of Christ and so betrays the faith evangelicals claim.

In 2015 the Southern Baptist Seminary and Association of Certified Biblical Counselors hosted a conference "to help the church respond in the present crisis" of what they called "transgenderism."[8] Fast-forward a decade later.

In the 2024 presidential election alone, Republicans spent $215 million in ads criticizing LGBTQ+ people.[9] These attack ads resonated with a pervasive conspiratorial suspicion of trans people—a minority of the US population—scapegoating them as the cause of American decline in many dimensions.

Consider that about 6.7 million trans people exist in America. It is an existence often marked by expulsion from family and community. I saw this ostracizing firsthand as a pastor. This means GOP spending in the 2024 election could be dispersed to about $30 for each trans citizen.[10] The stories told of trans people rendered them as a *threat* and helped curate the perceived "crisis" in both evangelicalism and conservatism together. Tragically, several mass shootings either perpetrated by a trans person or connected with fringes of trans ideology have come to speak for the whole. This perception is the product of propaganda. Made possible by a Department of Justice deleting credible studies that show political violence on the right outpaces all other ideological-based violence.[11]

Compare the evangelical definition of a "transgender crisis" to reports of a sexual abuse crisis in Southern Baptist institutions and churches. In 2007, *ABC News* published a report on abuse in the SBC.[12] In 2019, the *Houston Chronicle* released a six-part investigative series reporting over seven hundred cases of abuse in the SBC over a period of twenty years.[13]

In the years since, the SBC's efforts to address abuse were fractured by infighting—over how best to respond and in some cases whether the scandal was worthy of a "crisis" designation itself. This is the power of totality.

SBC churches voted to create a searchable database of abusers to make it easier to track predators moving between churches, but that plan was abandoned by executive leaders in order to recoup legal fees instead.[14] Defending these executive decisions was SBC executive and seminary president Jeff Iorg. Armed with data, he issued a defense of the SBC: "'Abuse is not frequently being reported in Southern Baptist churches,' Iorg told trustees. 'We have widely publicized this issue for the past five years and encouraged people to come forward with information and allegations. We now have verified, third-party data.' Because of this, he said, 'we reject the false narrative Southern Baptist churches are dangerous places for children. That Southern Baptists are protecting predators. And that Southern Baptists are uncaring in responding to survivors.' He added how 'with seven rare exceptions' among forty-seven thousand, Southern Baptist churches 'are cooperating to prevent abuse and address these [abuse] allegations.'"[15]

When the Department of Justice under Trump's second term ended its investigation of the SBC with only one arrest (a seminary official who forged records to mislead a federal investigation), the SBC leaders stepped up to claim vindication and revise the record. Denny Burk, a professor at Southern Baptist Seminary, said:

> So here's bottom line on the SBC abuse "crisis." There wasn't one. A federal investigation closed after making one arrest—not for abuse but for making false statements under oath. An independent investigation by Guidepost Solutions found no systemic problem with abuse at the SBC Executive Committee. We have spent about 14 million dollars in legal fees as a result of investigations that uncovered no systemic problems with abuse. The problem here is not with the good intentions of Southern Baptist messengers who were doing their level best to address a problem that was presented to them. The problem is with the

misinformation they were given about a "crisis" that in the end no one can find any evidence for.[16]

The different ways a "crisis of transgenderism" versus a crisis of abuse in churches plays out in evangelical institutions illuminate the way perception and storytelling determine how data is deployed in diverging ways, according to the demands of a totality. Everything depends on the story we tell. Especially when it comes to understanding the complexity of concrete human beings.

Facts and data—far from being unquestionable—often function as mere raw material selectively used to affirm (rather than challenge) the operative or prevailing totality and the stories that construct it. If you believe your perspective is "biblical" and your people are "right," then you can never be wrong—the danger, not just for practicing Christian faith but for our common life, is obvious.

A LOCALIZED APPROACH TO A LOOMING PROBLEM

So how do we stem the tide of so much *bad* information, when facts are insufficient in the face of totalities created by primal stories? As we said in the previous chapter: the crisis of storytelling demands a better story. But what does that look like? How do we move forward when the scale of the problem looms so large?

Asking that question involves solutions that can scale across societies and traverse the dimensions of digital space. But then there's the much smaller but no less significant dimension: the personal, the local. No one needs a degree, a credential, a platform to speak the truth. The Russian proverb is right: "One word of truth shall outweigh the whole world."[17]

In an excellent piece published in *Time* magazine, Sander van der Linden (professor of psychology at Cambridge) and Lee McIntyre (research fellow at the Center for Philosophy and History of Science at Boston University) both advocate for scalable ways to contend with information distortion while avoiding censorship. They argue, "Democracy doesn't function well when speech is exploited and manipulated to advance falsehoods. But fighting misinformation doesn't require censorship. In fact quite the opposite, it requires that we all speak out against it."[18] The irony is this: eliminating the category of disinformation itself ensures that censorship can continue insidiously and implicitly. When we no longer name the lie or falsehood, we give ourselves up to the tyranny of totality.

Democratic *access* to information is compatible with the pursuit of *accurate* information. That may be obvious to some, but in Disreality it needs to be said. When democracy is hollowed out, when our institutions, norms, and processes are seized by authoritarian interest and no longer represent the people, we can no longer assume a common reality that rests on commonly held facts and truth.

Now, we must ask again, where does democracy begin? How is it renewed? Faced with a problem of immense scale and scope, I want to suggest a localized approach to conspiracism and disinformation with our democratic interests in view. This approach becomes clear when we ask a different question: "How is disinformation being sustained among *this* group of people in *this* time and *this* place?"

This book focuses in on conspiracism in and across American evangelicalism. But it would be a mistake to assume evangelicalism has the corner on conspiracism. Especially if the driving motivation for that assumption is to generalize and pathologize, to shore up our own ideological defenses.

For example, in his book *The Rise of BlueAnon*, David Harsanyi documents what research confirms: there *are* unique forms of conspiracism more common to the American left—like 9/11-related conspiracies.[19] Unfortunately, many attempts to name conspiracism usually fall into ideological repartee. All they do, if they do anything, is shout, "Well, your side is worse!" Whataboutism cannot address this crisis. What is needed is truth-telling from within.

We are experiencing a great mainstreaming of conspiratorial belief. Disreality affects all of us, but it does so at the level of belonging. And to stay the tide of Disreality involves attending to the very beliefs that bind a certain community together. Holy paranoia is a totality that encloses evangelicalism. It reflects a unique on-ramp for conspiracism that actually transforms it into something theological, something to do with Jesus Christ and how evangelicals understand him.

On the way, however we define the term "evangelical," we will be confronted by a group of people who, in our moment, claim this label for themselves while displaying a marked affinity for varied conspiratorial beliefs held in tandem with and inseparable from Christian beliefs. To question one is to question another, with consequences for people who have never set foot in an evangelical congregation or political organization.

By focusing on the history of evangelical Christianity I am offering a way to contend with conspiracism from the ground up, rather than the top down. Both matter. But a localized approach to contending with conspiracy theory—especially among evangelicals—is better prepared to confront the theological crisis that rages alongside and ultimately beneath the surface crisis of conspiratorial thinking driving our political moment.

Fact-checking is vital, but it isn't enough to change anyone's mind when Christian faith is the backstop. I realized this as a pastor when I pressed certain facts among evangelicals, I was triggering a theological crisis alongside an epistemological one. Claims about Trump and Jesus were inseparable.

Story is why conspiracy theory retains its power when confronted with fact-checking activisms. Story sustains an ongoing answer to the question, how should we live? Not only does it sustain this answer, but story shapes this answer applied to every aspect of our lives, social, political, and beyond.

We need facts. Again, we shouldn't discredit them, but we can (and should) draw attention to their limits. And we do that by examining the primal stories that organize a community's totality.

TOTALITIES OF THE PARANOID

Because totalities are so intent on preserving their authority of truth, they have a tremendous capacity to hold paradoxical ideas, introducing paranoia—or split-mindedness—to the overarching story of that totality. Such is the case of Christian nationalism: a totalizing element that explicitly contradicts its central claims by elevating both fealty to country and fealty to Christ.

Consider the words of Eberhard Bethge. He was the close friend and confidant of the German pastor-theologian (and martyr) Dietrich Bonhoeffer, who died at the hands of the Nazis in the closing days of World War II.

Bethge was a witness and participant in the confessing church struggle inside Germany alongside Bonhoeffer. But he survived the war. Remarkably, he visited Jerry Falwell's Thomas Road Baptist Church in the 1980s at the height of the Moral Majority (a coalition of evangelical Christians organized as a key component of Ronald Reagan's presidential victory in 1980).

At his visit, Bethge was given two pins at the door. One, an American flag pin, the other, a "Jesus First!" pin. This is what he remembered, in his own words:

> I couldn't help but think of myself in Germany in 1933. That was exactly what we believed . . . on the one hand, our nation's proud renewal, to which we wanted to devote our energy and time and to make sacrifices if need be; on the other hand, to be devoted to Jesus Christ at the same time. Why not that relation and that equation? Then I remembered that slow and bitter revelation how in the interpretation, even in that "Jesus First," the flag in fact became the guiding force. Of course, Christ, but a German Christ; of course, "Jesus First," but an American Jesus! And so to the long history of faith and of its executors another chapter is being added of a mixed image of Christ.[20]

This anecdote is personal. Because *I* served at this very church. Bethge's prophetic warning of mixing patriotism and faith has gone largely unheeded. In my time at Liberty and Thomas Road during the Obama presidency, the same sort of nationalistic fervor was the *norm*.

Before we draw too fine an analogy between our time and 1930s Germany, we should recall that this *exact* sort of "paranoid" Jesus was recognized generations earlier among the enslaved in America, too. This paranoid "mixed-image" of Christ was on the mind of the great orator, reverend, and abolitionist Frederick Douglass, when he wrote,

> Between the Christianity of this land, and the Christianity of Christ, I recognize the widest possible difference—so wide, that to receive the one as good, pure, and holy, is of necessity to reject the other as bad, corrupt, and wicked. To be the friend of the one, is of necessity to be the enemy of the other. I love the pure, peaceable, and impartial Christianity of Christ: I therefore hate the corrupt, slaveholding, women-whipping, cradle-plundering, partial and hypocritical Christianity of this land. Indeed, I can see no reason, but the most deceitful one, for calling the religion of this land Christianity. I look upon it as the climax of all misnomers, the boldest of all frauds, and the grossest of all libels. Never was there a clearer case of "stealing the livery of the court of heaven to serve the devil in."[21]

This story of America contained in and rehearsed by the totality of white evangelicalism has theological consequences. The blending of one story with the Christian story curates a perception that deals with facts differently, and ultimately renders a different sort of Christ at the heart of evangelical Christianity in America. This paranoid Jesus makes it so that this telling of a story about America isn't just historically wrong, but heretically dangerous.

When holding a "biblical worldview" commits you to a sanitized myth of America, you are operating in a sort of epistemological totalitarianism. Nothing can be more dangerous than assuming you have the full scope of things from a position that is obscured or, worse, distorted. The conceit of evangelicalism is retreating into the adjective "biblical" as a shelter from accountability and inquiry.

I'm not saying evangelicals are ignorant. I'm saying that by stretching the primal truth of Christian confession over and across all fields of knowledge and calling that operation a "biblical worldview," evangelicals have constructed a self-justifying totality. A sanitized myth of America smuggled into a Christian story shapes a perception that is both dangerous for common political life and marked by denial of the reality that is Jesus.

A CHRISTIAN AMERICA

In his study of Israel's ancient prophets, theologian Walter Brueggemann says the prophetic task of Christian community takes on three dimensions: telling the truth, grieving, and curating hope.[22]

White Christians in America have abandoned these tasks, rehearsing stories in and about America that have determined and framed and warped our theology and perpetuated injustice.

These stories, just as much as the embrace of spurious facts, are a prime source for our conspiratorially charged world. These stories curate perceptions that develop an affinity for conspiratorial claims, ones that cast evangelicals as the righteous against "the left."

I think to see and understand the popularity of conspiracy theory among evangelicals has to do with what the Christian story has become in the hands of evangelicals *in America*. This telling of the Christian story has become indistinguishable from and bound up in a sanitized telling of the American story.

There is no one authorized telling of the American story. And yet, the totality that organizes evangelicalism in America retains and rehearses a sanitized and exclusive telling of the American story, set alongside the Christian story. Claims like the Founding Fathers were all practicing evangelical Christians, while they cut against the grain of disciplined historical research, go a long way in offering moral justification to authoritarian politics.

When one story is folded into another, the prophetic truth of Christian faith is silenced and made to serve the needs and necessities of the American Empire. We could almost invert Brueggemann's observation. In telling a Christianized story of America, evangelical churches are primed to promote propaganda deepening society's illusion, practice denial as a way to avoid lament and repentance, and conceive of hope in terms of the nation, not the Kingdom.

Every church in America, simply by virtue of existing and witnessing to the gospel of Jesus, tells a story about America. Not every telling of the story is the same; except that in its telling there come consequences. It's not just that these stories alter or shape or express the theology evangelicals confess; it's also that this story determines what political or moral action looks like in the world.

But, where does the story of America start? And who gets to tell it? These are far from settled questions, yet evangelicalism prefers to explicitly tell or tacitly promote a set and sanitized story of America, one purged of its uncomfortable facts and primed to promote the supremacy of Christians above all else. This storied myth centers a specific Christian experience and expectation over and above other possibilities.

I found this to be true as a pastor in a particular time and place. It was a place that made it possible to tell the story of America from a sole street corner. That corner is Caroline Street and William Street in Fredericksburg, Virginia. But the problem, I quickly discovered, was that my own community was trafficking in a different story, one of denial, that made it impossible to consider any other telling, not just as a matter of "revisionist history" but as a matter of Christian faith.

By couching calls to deeper racial awareness as "social justice" or "DEI" and so evidence of spiritual backsliding, some tellings of the American story are treated as more decidedly "Christian" in the evangelical world, I found.

But it is still possible to stand at the corner of Caroline and William Streets and hear a different story, one that disrupts the sense that "good Christians" only tell a preapproved story of America, one that keeps you on good terms with evangelicalism and its political goals.

Look around. Because other stories are all around us.

If you stood at the corner of Caroline and William today, I'd point you first to the site where General Weedon's Tavern stood before it burned down in 1807. I'd tell you about the owner of the tavern, Weedon, a veteran of the French and Indian War and a general in the American Revolutionary Army. He owned and operated this modest tavern in Fredericksburg. Soon, it outgrew its modesty.

During the revolution, the tavern established itself as a veritable hub for patriotic zeal. Weedon was host to the likes of George Washington, Patrick Henry, and Thomas Jefferson. Conversation went on between cards, and continued with successive stays for nights on end. After the French American victory at Yorktown that turned the world upside down, Weedon decided to plan a peace ball, which was attended by Washington and Frenchman Marquis de Lafayette, who arrived with Mary Washington, the mother of George Washington.

The tavern, which no longer stands, wasn't just a host for political conversation. It was a site of national significance.

In 1777, Thomas Jefferson arrived with fellow delegates of the newly independent Commonwealth of Virginia and made the tavern a working office. The men labored incessantly to update and revise legal codes for a free Virginia. Among the decisions made by these men in the upstairs confines of Weedon's Tavern was drafting the slave codes that protected the institution of chattel slavery, including laws designed to prevent slave insurrection. Jefferson's Virginia made it illegal for enslaved people to meet without their master present.

In 1862, over two hundred thousand Union and Confederate soldiers clashed at this corner and in the streets of Fredericksburg over the question of slavery. The corner of Caroline and William was the site of vicious urban combat. Nearly twenty thousand men were killed, wounded, or missing over the course of the battle.

By 1960, the site of the tavern had been replaced with a diner, Woolworths. It was here, on the very site where Thomas Jefferson wrote Virginia's slave codes, where ancestors of the enslaved and their allies staged sit-ins protesting Jim Crow segregation two centuries later.

The protestors at Woolworths and another cafe across

the street defied Fredericksburg segregation laws, in challenges to Jim Crow that were erupting beyond the small town across America. Fast-forward sixty years in the same streets of Fredericksburg with a site of Black Lives Matter protests, the very community where I was a pastor.

I had many conversations in the summer of 2020 about the legacy of racism, not just in America writ large, but in our community. Our pastoral staff meetings were filled with talk about racism and the need for "reconciliation" (language that problematically assumes equal responsibility in contributing to the problem of racism, and which in white spaces amounted to an event, a spectacle of prayer that enabled us to return to our segregated communities without a sense of responsibility toward reparation). Any more than this, and the line was crossed; there was space to discuss until it was no longer "in the interest of unity" to continue talking about such "divisive" topics like race.

The church where I was a pastor in 2020, like most white, upper-middle-class, conservative evangelical churches in America, offered little resistance to the white cultural backlash to Black Lives Matter. Our church apologized publicly for attending a prayer gathering of local churches to address racism and police brutality. The reason was partisan optics: a sign stating "Black Lives Matter" was visible in a photo uploaded to church socials. The ethos of "thin blue line" won out over everything. And it was this backlash that was, at the same time, coalescing in renewed support for Donald Trump's 2020 campaign.

Make no mistake, in these churches, you would still hear slogans in opposition to racism. But it was racism that was only conceived in terms of individual and, therefore, personal hatred and animosity. There was no room for considering racism as a fully grown material and structural system of oppression that permeates every area of American life. To talk this way, to think this way, was to be labeled a "cultural Marxist"—which, of course, I was in those summer months.

Beyond fact checks, we need renewed attention to the primal stories that converge and contradict on the way to constructing totality. And you do not know these stories or how they interact without entering and participating in the common life of a community. Upending totalities can only be done from within. That's what happened with me.

I'll never forget a conversation I had that summer with a pastor I had served with. He had lived in Fredericksburg for over thirty years. We were talking about the half-century history of the church, and about the need to update the church constitution. Particularly we were talking about the fact that the church's constitution (unchanged since 1956) made no mention of race, showed no written resistance to Jim Crow segregation, and that this omission in light of current events was telling.

He dismissed that view, remarking, "Well, we don't know

how bad it was here." Except that, if we had bothered to read the signs, bothered to hear stories outside of our own telling of the American story, then perhaps our faith would have looked and lived different in our time, too.

I didn't always think that way. I made friends in New Orleans whose lives, the very texture of their entire existence, forced me to reconsider some of my deepest assumptions about America and a Christian faith committed to its ordering.

Totality necessitates a forgetting that is dangerous. Which is why I think we need to go deeper. Not just into the tellings of an American story in service of white supremacy, but also looking at the stories evangelicals tell about ourselves. Specifically the untold history of the way conspiracy theory has served us across three centuries in America.

Chapter 3

AN UNTOLD STORY

Memory is a moral exercise.

—Stanley Hauerwas, *The Peaceable Kingdom*

In 1960, Republican candidate Barry Goldwater was making a run for the presidency. In many ways, Goldwater was a harbinger of MAGA, a prototype of Trump. He cast his enemies as communists; his campaign played loose with conspiratorial accusations. He lost the race, but made his mark on the political right in America by perfecting what scholar Richard Hofstadter named "the paranoid style."

The paranoid style was an aesthetic, an ethos, a carefully curated vibe, animating a dangerous sort of politics practiced by the right in Cold War America. He described this style as the sort of politics that relied less on the difference between truth and falsehood or fact and fiction, but more on the feelings of persecution, and the need to defeat a common enemy. Sound familiar?

The Cold War set the stage for this paranoid style, with its anxiety over communist infiltration. The "Red Scare" of the early fifties not only organized American politics, but it shaped the everyday American social psyche. America tried to *resolve* Cold War anxiety through telling stories, too.

The stories America told during the Cold War were deeply saturated by the anxieties of their time. The paranoid style was bound up in this moment. Those cheap 1950s alien flicks? *Creature from the Black Lagoon*? All that weird sci-fi? Those B movies and radio serials weren't just offering everyday Americans an escape from their anxieties, they were attempts to resolve them.

Cold War America processed its collective fear of communist infiltration partly through producing and consuming stories of alien invasions. America has always done this: looking to story to name and resolve the contradictions of our time, and reestablish our identity as "the good guys." Not unlike how the ancient Romans relied on the myths of the gods.

George Lucas's *Star Wars* resolved the anxieties of a new generation of Americans who were embattled by acting like the Empire in Vietnam, longing to be the Rebels once again. Later still, in 2008, when Robert Downey Jr. walked out of a cave of Islamic jihadists in Afghanistan wearing Iron Man's first suit, this imagery was a bid to soothe the American anxiety over terrorism and the public divide over the War on Terror. The power of story goes on.

And so, just as the same way cheap B-movie alien stories and *Star Wars* fit the time they were in, so did the Christian story in the hands of evangelicals across American history, including the Cold War.

The more Hofstadter examined the paranoid style in Cold War America, the closer he got to identifying its source. He concluded, "the evangelical movement has been the most powerful carrier of this kind of religious anti-intellectualism."[1] This was a half century ago. Disreality now emerges from a past that evangelicalism tends to either deny or distort.

WILL THE REAL EVANGELICAL PLEASE STAND UP?

There is no authorized definition of "evangelical" or official story of evangelicalism. There is no single evangelical denomination, no central magisterial authority, like in the Roman Catholic or Orthodox churches. You do not need a membership card to be an evangelical. You can really just step out there and claim it.

Some suggest the evangelical label is *ideally* a theological term, a label reserved for those who subscribe to a package of Christian beliefs summed up by something called Bebbington's quadrilateral.[2] This is a concept invented by historian David Bebbington. It's a package deal of four theological

"-isms" he calls "crucicentrism" or belief in the Cross, "conversionism" or belief in a transformational experience of conversation or being "born again," "biblicism" or emphasis on the Bible, and finally "activism" or the insistence on moral behavior across society. But this doesn't fully explain *why* people flock to the label.

Daniel Silliman tried to use these four beliefs to understand how the evangelical magazine *Christianity Today* was founded. This was his conclusion:

> The real meaning of "evangelical" would always be contested. It would be in flux. What is interesting, though, is that the Bebbington quadrilateral does not explain that flux. Focus on a moment in history when evangelicals are defining evangelicalism, drawing lines, and making decisions about who they trust, and the four marks do not explain why they do any of the things they do.[3]

Claiming to be "evangelical" is now more aligned with one's support for Trump than anything else, including one's faith. This shift toward a partisan label gives rise to a strange phenomenon: a Buddhist evangelical or even a nonreligious evangelical.[4] This might strike us as strange until we recognize how "evangelical" has become more a partisan signifier than a Christian one. There are those for whom "evangelical" will always refer to a decidedly Christian confession or set of beliefs. But increasingly, the label is used to indicate what sort of policy or conservative ideology one might carry into the political stream.

This matters. How people define or claim "evangelical" ends up rendering a host of stories that (when you start to compare them) are wildly contradictory. Take January 6, 2021. If you define "evangelical" by a theological definition, say the Bebbington quadrilateral, well, you might look at the prayers and the protests and the violence of the Capitol Insurrection and conclude: "These people aren't *real* evangelicals." And the quadrilateral might help you reach that conclusion.

Surveying the events of January 6 (and the cultural memory that emerged to alter, mythologize, and revise it), the Bebbington quadrilateral would have us look for evidence of beliefs like "crucicentrism"—do they believe in the primacy of the Cross? Or "conversionism"—do they believe in a "born again" faith? My point here is to suggest how arbitrary these metrics are while, at the same time, drawing attention to the moral power involved in using these metrics to disregard or distort evangelical involvement in and influence on January 6.

These theological frameworks used to define "evangelical" can just as easily serve as elaborate schemes of denial, as they do definition. Applied to January 6, it may be just as easy to claim those weren't "real" evangelicals.

The consequence of this casual write-off is that one is

let off the hook, no longer responsible for dealing with the Christian symbolism and imagery of January 6. No one has to take responsibility if they aren't "our" type of evangelical.

See, it's not just the story evangelicals tell about America that counts. It's also the stories evangelicals tell about themselves. These stories can become shelters that hide evangelicals away from the God they claim to confess and bear witness to.

When I began my research into conspiracism, I started not with the claims of conspiracies but with the stories of evangelicalism. What I found was a steady stream of conspiratorial narration across the span of American history. Like the way evangelical revivalists before the Revolution pacified white fears of slave revolts, or how antisemitic conspiracies were commonly involved in preaching and evangelical publications in the early twentieth century, not to mention the present time of MAGA Christianity. This led me to a simple conclusion.

There isn't a single period of evangelical history when conspiracy theory isn't doing some kind of work for evangelicals.

Now, the work is varied. Sometimes, conspiracy gives their message a sense of urgency, like when revivalists in revolutionary America preached to pacify revolts and resistance from enslaved people. Other times, conspiracy gives the gospel relevancy, like when Billy Graham promised Americans that mass conversion to Christianity would stave off the communist menace infiltrating America. Other times, conspiracy *extends* the message itself, like on January 6, when claims of a stolen election were received as content on par with the message.

The historical legacy of evangelicalism and conspiracy theory matters for today if only because this legacy is incredibly varied. Conspiracy theory, it turns out, has many uses. It's not just that it promises the ultimate way to "know" things. Conspiracy theory also emerges from social, political, and existential situations that have—in turn—shaped the evangelical tradition in America itself. Whether framing revival preaching or political activism, conspiracy theory is a constant feature of evangelical preaching and politics in America. This history matters. And it's largely a history evangelicals are willfully ignorant over.

Why go through this history? I get it. Few of us need any reminders of the pain and persistence of conspiracy theory. But this untold history shows us three things. First, it reminds us that nothing about the *presence* of conspiracy theory entangled in faith is a *new* creation. Second, it helps us recognize the way(s) conspiracy theory reflects a deeper theological crisis raging beneath evangelical Christianity in America. But third, based on that recognition, it also helps us identify who is at risk under the prevailing attitudes and actions that this sort of conspiracism curates. This matters as citizens, whether you're a Christian, evangelical, or not.

The paranoia over revolts led by enslaved people, the

anxiety over communist infiltration, and the existential fears of a deep state all have shaped evangelical theology and praxis in significant ways up to the present. The key to understanding (and more importantly dismantling) this influence is acknowledging that conspiracism is itself the window into this house, not necessarily the house itself. The crisis of conspiracism in Christian community emerges from theological malpractice and the malformation it causes.

This chapter compiles this untold history in a series of episodes. Each homes in on acute holy paranoia in that era. Each account is paired with some analysis, breaking down the history and examining its relationships. And both account and analysis converge in a final section that addresses what this means for Christian belief and life.

In all this, we need to say, again, that the prominence and popularity of conspiratorial narratives in themselves do not mark out evangelicals as actually that much different from many Americans who also trafficked in particular conspiracies about specific historical events, like the JFK assassination.

America is the land of conspiracy theory. We love them. And there's something perhaps unique to our collective social consciousness that makes America so anxious of shadowy institutions and elites. By looking at this untold history of conspiracism in and across evangelical Christianity in America, we come to see the ways conspiratorial narration and suspicion shapes and corrupts the theology that fuels a paranoid Christian witness.

So this is a dangerous chapter.

Not just because this chapter unveils the untold story of evangelical conspiracism. But also because of the minefield of assumptions we have to negotiate and navigate to make it through.

The stories we tell—and the stories we don't—have moral power. We've been singing this song in melody and harmony, across many different keys, for most of the book so far. And now we come to a really crucial point: the stories evangelicals tell about ourselves are a window into the holy paranoia that so marks the movement in this moment.

The guild of evangelical historians and its ever-evolving consensus on what constitutes evangelical identity illustrate something much more dynamic than four beliefs. Those beliefs can organize and tell one story, but it will inevitably leave something out.

This is why I'm most interested in the power invested and authority involved in telling the evangelical story. The stakes of this storytelling act are just as consequential for the conspiracy theories given safe harbor in evangelicalism. Why? Because attention to conspiracy theories across evangelical history shows a long-running affinity for conspiratorial tropes and narratives.

Defining "evangelical" and telling this story often serves

as a scheme of justification—a way to defend one group of people by creating distance from others. And when it comes to naming and resisting the conspiratorial gospel, we cannot disregard the *way* the evangelical story is told. Precisely because, told in service of evangelicals, evangelical history functions as a no-true-Scotsman in constant flux.

But here's the danger. It would be easy—too easy—for me to trot out all the historical facts and evidence of conspiracism across evangelical history. I could leave us with the idea (either implicitly or explicitly) that each and every evangelical you meet is a "conspiracy theorist" of the highest order. I could imply every evangelical church is so saturated by conspiratorial beliefs that none of them should be taken seriously.

Historically, conspiracy theory has been a load-bearing wall in the structure of evangelicalism from era to era. But the point of this chapter is to show how the stories evangelicals themselves tell about evangelicals in America are dangerously incomplete. Dangerous, because edited histories, omitted episodes, an emphasis placed at *this* figure rather than *that* one, all of these moves go a long way in constructing a history that, in many cases, functions as a scheme of sanction, of self-justification.

These forgotten dimensions of evangelical history (stories that are always being told and retold) show the way in which conspiracism continues to sit at the heart of evangelicalism, ready to seize upon and serve the needs of the totality of holy paranoia. Whether or not an individual evangelical defines themself as a conspiracy theorist is secondary to the more primary question of why conspiratorial thinking is so commonplace across evangelicalism in America.

Laying out these episodes isn't my way of condemning evangelical Christians as an entire community of conspiracy theorists. The point of this chapter is to recount the untold history of conspiracism within evangelical Christianity to suggest that perhaps the way forward demands the disruption of holy paranoia.

WITCHES AND CHRISTIAN HYSTERIA

The first "conspiracy theorists" in America were a group of people known as the Puritans.[5] While explaining this group would have us delving back into the historical contexts of England and even the Reformation, we have to skip over that bit to get to more pressing issues.

In short, the Puritans came to the shores of North America seeking room to practice what, in modern terms, could be called authoritarian Christendom. It was, in a modern sense, its own form of totalitarianism. The Puritan pastor and politician Cotton Mather wrote that the Puritans fled European persecution for the "new world" and arrived in "the Devil's territories" where "it may easily be supposed that the Devil was exceedingly disturbed, when he perceived such a People here accomplishing the Promise of old made unto our Blessed Jesus."[6]

While the tidy myths of American history tend to cast the Puritans as victims of religious wars in Europe, specifically in England, Scotland, Ireland, and Wales, they were not quite as idyllic and innocent as curriculum tends to suggest. Not only did the Puritans arrive on land that was not theirs, but they had also exhibited a penchant for authoritarian political projects back home.

In fact, the Puritans, exemplified best by the likes of Oliver Cromwell, fomented Civil War and led England into an experiment with republican government. Puritans not only aimed to reform the Church of England away from Roman Catholicism, they also saw that effort as part of a broader political project of coercive conformity to their Christian ideal. This is looking backward.

Looking ahead, in terms of American history, it is also accurate to say that the Puritans who arrived on American shores are "proto-evangelicals." The Puritans came to American shores as part of a settler colonial project involving the expansion of England's mercantile empire under the pretext that they were a persecuted minority, when in fact they had upturned and overturned the political order of England for a time.

They founded Massachusetts as an attempt to create a new "city on a hill"—an experiment in Christendom as a totalitarian, church-driven society. In some versions of the colonial constitution, the fullest political rights were reserved for church members.

Generations later, the legacy of the Puritans in North America would influence some of the key American evangelicals of revolutionary America, like Jonathan Edwards. All this might sound oddly similar to efforts of Christian nationalists today. For our purposes, all of this is critical background material. Because it was in the heart of this Puritan society in New England where evangelical conspiracism began to take shape: the Salem witch trials.

The Salem witch trials began in 1692. The events that led to the trials and executions of women actually started in the household of a Salem reverend.[7] This point of origin is significant. Because most insular, totalitarian societies assume the existence of external threats. Great energy and effort are expanded in that direction. But internal threats are even more dangerous to the stability of these coercive regimes. When the reverend reported fits and seizures among his children, these events were quickly interpreted as the result of witchcraft performed by enslaved persons in his house.[8] Over the next several months, both ministers and officials across New England were drawn into, and perhaps stoked, a hysteria over witches who had supposedly infiltrated Puritan society.

It's significant that the blame fell on the enslaved and women, fitting for a patriarchal society driven in part by the economy of chattel slavery. In June, Bridget Bishop, a woman, was the first to be executed. Ten more would follow in the coming months. John Russell Smith, writing two hundred years later, notes that even two dogs were put to death on suspicion of giving safe harbor to schemes of the Devil.[9] As the panic ensued, accusations of witchcraft reached from the commons to official institutions and then to skeptics, who were doubtful over the legitimacy of this obvious social contagion.

To quell the crisis, Governor Phips asked a Puritan minister, Cotton Mather, to pen the government's (at that time, the Massachusetts Bay Colony) account of the trials.[10] This would perhaps provide closure to the hysteria, as well as legitimize the proceedings, sanitizing them in Spiritual language.

What's interesting is how Mather's explanation of the Salem witch trials mirrors the conspiratorial narration so popular among evangelicals today. His narration drew heavily from accounts of angels, demons, and Satan, in ways similar to the modern evangelical invocation of the demonic to account for things like mask mandates or stolen elections.

In the account, Mather charged Satan and his legions with the assault on Puritan society through the demonic use of female bodies. Mather explained his motivations in the introduction: "I have indeed set myself to countermine the whole PLOT of the Devil, against New-England."[11] For Mather, the trials of Salem represented nothing less than the government's counterattack to what was nothing short of a supernatural assault by Satan and demons on the Christian purity of New England society.

The reactionary move to blame the Devil on the disruption is a common tactic still deployed in Christian PR management today. Especially in the wake of scandals within churches. Because the anxiety seemed to emerge from within Puritan society, and not outside of it, Mather had to reach into the supernatural realm to locate the apparent source of the affliction. The use of demonic categories for Mather allowed him to resolve the contradiction. For example, Mather derived *proof* of Puritan supremacy and purity from the satanic assault itself. This reflects a long-standing belief of Mather's, one evidenced by his decision to quote English theologian Richard Baxter in the foreword to an earlier work of his on witchcraft: "Where will the Devil show most Malice, but where he is hated, and hateth most."[12] The assumed "purity" of Puritan society, as with many fundamentalist, insular communities, is always perceived to be at risk from external invasion, and rarely internal infiltration.

Mather's account reinforced the notion that, in spite of the fact that the hysteria emerged from within the community, they were still righteous and pure.[13] During the hysteria, Mather constantly upheld this purity of New England society and juxtaposed it with Satan's invasive schemes that he impressed onto the bodies of the enslaved and women. It is a recurring theme throughout Mather's account.

Just like Mather reached for the demonic within the

confines of Puritanical society, so many evangelicals grasp after the "demonic" deep state in their conspiratorial narrations in our contemporary moment. Alongside this demonic narration is also the willingness to code the bodies of women and marginalized people as the "source" of national decline or risk. Whereas in Mather's day, this coding involved the bodies of women, the enslaved, and Indigenous Americans, in our day, we must also include the panic associated with the perceived "impurity" of queer bodies, whose mere existence is often perceived as an existential threat in and of itself. We'll return to the demonic coding of marginalized bodies. There is more history to uncover.

PACIFYING PREACHERS: SLAVERY AND WHITE ANXIETY

Forty years after the Salem witch trials, the British colonies on American shores were an essential economic factor in the ascendant power of the British Empire. One of the essential economic cogs in this imperial machine was the slave trade. And so, for a social order designed to serve the economic interests of the empire, it was essential for relationships between the enslaved and those who claimed ownership over their bodies to exist in a state of relative peace.

This overpowering social and economic reality is often, curiously, absent or downplayed in many accounts of the origins of evangelicalism in America. These origins are usually located in an event (or really series of events) across several years, taking place across the transatlantic world, up and down the colonies of British America and in the United Kingdom itself. It was a revival movement that came to be known as "The Great Awakening"—a term that, incidentally enough, QAnon has seized for its own conspiratorial prophetic canon. More on that in a bit.

When it comes to the origins of evangelicalism in America, great pains are taken to map the theological distinctions of evangelicals from their Catholic or establishment counterparts. The works of esteemed theologian Jonathan Edwards are consulted, often at the expense of questions concerning his status as a slaveholder.

The great revivalist George Whitefield, a man whom even Benjamin Franklin traveled to hear speak, shook the American colonists from New England down to Georgia. Even so, Whitefield was a man who, though staunchly committed to the Church of England, advocated for the extension and existence of chattel slavery on the grounds that God might use it providentially to bring the gospel to enslaved people.

In short, to examine the origins of evangelicals in America without attention to slavery is to fail to tell the story in its fullness. Their theological projects cannot be understood *apart* from the social and political orders that shaped their worlds, and the economic logics that drove their expansion. Once we adjust for this, we come to find that a key forgotten element of the Great Awakening revivals was the evangelical maintenance of the economic institution of chattel slavery.

This commitment to chattel slavery meant, among other things, the domestication of the Christian gospel to stave off the anxiety that every white landowning man in America felt in his bones: the fear of armed revolts by the enslaved. And indeed, though evangelicals were mavericks in their desire to preach to the enslaved, the Great Awakening revivals only ever reified the economic logic of slavery and so sought to pacify white anxiety of revolts, the conspiracy theory that often came true.

Like it did in 1739, when a man known to history by the name of Cato led an armed uprising of enslaved people in the colony of South Carolina. Timing the uprising on Sunday, when their masters would be in church, Cato and his fellow liberators armed themselves and fought their way through white resistance. It took a few hours before a larger white militia could be formed, which eventually surrounded Cato's men and killed them.

Such revolts were a constant source of anxiety for white slave owners and the entire American South. And Cato's uprising, what came to be known as the Stono Rebellion, confirmed the suspicions of white anxiety. It was palpable, and ever-present. And so preventative measures were taken. Such measures included arming slave owners while denying arms to the enslaved. But also, and significantly, it often included ensuring a lack of literacy coupled with the refusal to teach and preach Christianity to the enslaved. These measures, however, seemed to be threatened and paradoxically reinforced all at the same time during a widespread evangelical revival that swept through the American colonies.

A few decades before the American Revolution, there was an American revival. Today, scholars call it the "Great Awakening." Over about a decade, itinerant preachers and American pastors gathered large crowds in pastures and pulpits. They preached passionately, directly to the heart. But they also were excellent promoters and publicists. Because of mass-market printing, it was easier than ever for churches in the United Kingdom and the American colonies to report back to each other on what they described as great moves of God.

But printed pamphlets were not the only cargo crossing the Atlantic. People were, too. The economic institution of chattel slavery was an essential part of the colonial social order. And it was a social order that thought of itself—before, during, and after the revivals—as distinctively Christian. The revivals did little to change or question this social order, even if they redrew boundaries between churches and Christian institutions and inflamed in colonists a new zeal and passion.

Historians remain divided as to why these revivals were so successful. Ironically, this fault line reflects what people at the time of the revivals felt about them, too.

Some were (and are) quick to attribute the popular revival to promotion, to special techniques of public speaking, to basically material factors. The Great Awakening was an invention, as historian Frank Lambert argues, one that relied on the mastery of the printing press and transatlantic publishing networks.[14] Others look less to the material factors, and more to what they recognize as spiritual factors. They focus on the doctrine of the preachers, the content of the sermons, and the writings of their followers.

Why were the revivals so successful? One reason is how the social and political world was primed for this sort of preaching. It was a preaching aimed at people who sat in church every week, people who performed the social scripts of Christianized societies, but perhaps were not Christian themselves.

In a powerful insight, historian Andrew Walls observes, this evangelicalism assumed Christendom.[15] The founding impulse of evangelical Christianity in America is reliant on the realization of Christian supremacy in the political.[16]

By "Christendom" I mean the long-standing integration of church with state, as practiced in America by the Puritans. Or, put more conceptually, Christendom is the way Western Christianity exerted influence on and integrated with the social, economic, and political development of Europe, including colonization. When the revivals began, they were directed at people who, simply by virtue of their being born under the reign of a British king, would likely have called themselves "Christian."

And so the Great Awakening was a call to "authentic" faith beneath the prevailing and dominating social structures and political institutions of the day that went by the name "Christian." By assuming Christendom, evangelicalism also assumed the social order. And so it isn't surprising that conspiracy theories about threats to that social order played heavily into revival preaching. And in the British colonies, there was no greater threat than the enslaved seeking their liberation.

The social anxiety of white colonists over a potential uprising of enslaved people would, in many ways, come to frame the preaching of the Great Awakening itself. To see how this happened, we have to focus on particular figures.

The revivals were so public and influential that preachers soon began to take on the form of what we'd probably call celebrities today. George Whitefield was one such figure. Some scholars today call Whitefield an "agent of Empire." And it's easy to see why. Whitefield was an Anglican minister (of the Church of England) who traveled broadly across the British world. He studied at Oxford alongside the Wesley brothers, who would go on to found the Methodist Church. And both Whitefield and the Wesleys would travel widely, from Britain to the Caribbean, the American colonies, and back again. The scope of their travels was matched only by the scale of the crowds that gathered to hear them. Even Benjamin Franklin was impressed by Whitefield when he came to Philadelphia.

Whitefield's impact in America centers on his ministry in the South, particularly in Georgia, where he founded Bethesda, an orphanage meant to support his missionary work. But Bethesda proved difficult to maintain. And Whitefield soon began to advocate for the expansion of chattel slavery as a way to fix the labor problems with his institution. The economic questions made slavery an attractive prospect for Whitefield, who often argued that because enslaved people came to hear the gospel that God was using the institution for his own purposes.

Whitefield endorsed chattel slavery for economic purposes. And it was his twisted, rigid Calvinism that allowed him to justify the brutal exploitation of black bodies in the belief that God's providence brought them to America to hear the gospel and so be saved. In this twisted scheme of salvation, Whitefield diverged from many preachers who refused to preach to the enslaved. Whitefield addressed the enslaved directly with a domesticating gospel. This practice was enough to fuel anxiety among the white population, who felt *any* sort of Christianity among the enslaved would result in uprisings. And so, Whitefield promoted a particularly domesticating, moralizing gospel that bound the enslaved to their white masters in the name of Christ. Still, the anxieties could not be abated and conspiracy theories persisted.

In 1742, just three years removed from Stono, one Charleston newspaper wrote that Whitefield's preaching together with evangelical pamphlets sweeping across the colonies were "filling [enslaved people's] heads with a parcel of cant-phrases, trances, visions, and revolutions, and something still worse, and which Prudence forbids to name."[17] The "worse" that could not be printed was the potent white anxiety over another Stono.

Whitefield responded to this charge in his ministry by constantly assuring the slave owners he was one of them. In preaching to the enslaved, as he continued to do, in his own words he credited God for enabling him "to touch the negroes, and yet not to give them the least umbrage to slight or behave imperviously to their masters."[18] In all this, Whitefield catered to the anxieties of the slaveholder—and his conspiratorial anxieties over a slave revolt—more than the emancipatory rights of the enslaved.

Whitefield advocated for slavery, and benefited economically from it. The wider British Christianized social order and its economic system was not something Whitefield was interested in changing. In fact, Whitefield's political advocacy was in expanding slavery. Though Whitefield's preaching startled slave owners, his actual message was not one of liberation, but pacification.

It's worth mentioning here that not all evangelicals fell in line behind Whitefield. Those who did framed their gospel in ways that sought to reinforce the social order. But not all took this path. Significantly, Whitefield and Wesley had a major theological disagreement that forever altered their ministry collaboration. The theological dimensions here are too great to recount in detail, but it centered on the question of God's sovereignty.

Whitefield, who defended chattel slavery on the grounds that God used it to sovereignly preach the gospel to the enslaved, argued God's sovereignty was deterministic, and fated. Men and women could not change their destiny. If they had been chosen for damnation, that was that. Wesley, on the other hand, argued that men and women could indeed exercise their agency and choose salvation. This disagreement marked a theological and political divergence. Wesley became deeply involved in public abolitionism, and his influence is largely credited with the dissolution of the slave trade in the UK some forty years before America settled the question with a bloody Civil War.

But in America, evangelicalism went in a different direction. Though there were dissenters and divergences,[19] the popular development of evangelical Christianity in America threaded a needle. On the one hand, Whitefield and his followers were criticized by slave owners for fomenting insurrection simply by preaching to slaves. This accusation, in turn, put the burden on Whitefield and his fellow preachers to prove that their preaching pacified the enslaved, and made them more docile in the name of Jesus.

Evangelicals like Whitefield exhibited a preferential option for the white Christian slave owner. This meant (among other things) that the conspiratorial anxiety of southern societies over revolts found its way into the preaching of

Whitefield and his followers. While arguing that their preaching to the enslaved was not at all insurrectionary, Whitefield and his followers quickly seized on the potency of white anxiety as a way to scale their preaching for mass appeal and conversion.

For example, Hugh Bryan, in a sermon to the residents of Charleston, South Carolina, leveraged the widespread conspiratorial panic over revolts to add a sense of urgency and legitimacy to his gospel preaching. He warned that, unless the city repented, perhaps the rumors of enslaved meetings on the outskirts of the city had a divine purpose. Perhaps, unless Charleston repented, God would unleash "African Hosts" to judge the city.[20] This "conspiracy-busting" gospel remains popular today.

The conspiratorial anxiety over revolts from enslaved people framed the way Great Awakening revivalists connected with their audience and drove home the call to repentance. But in these narrations that made use of conspiratorial anxiety, they never suggested freedom for the enslaved. By presenting the Christian gospel as one with "conspiracy-busting power," the Great Awakening evangelicals across the slaveholding South presented a god on the side of the slave owner. A god who might allow the presumably "demonic" or "evil" threat of social upheaval to judge the equally presumptuous, righteous slave-owning masters. This was a repentance to God that also promised the preservation of social order.

If we think that this sort of framing ended with the eradication of slavery, we'd be wrong. The basic framework of a conspiracy-busting gospel to assuage conspiratorial anxiety is with us still. The basic impulse that a revival will also reinstate the social order is, at its most basic form, the continuation of this legacy. It can be found in 2020, in the sermons of John MacArthur, particularly one called "Who's to Blame for the Riots?" He said, "If we go back to the Word of God, back to ordered families, back to just government, back to sound faithful godly churches, it can change. Apart from that, it grows worse, until we are taken, the final restraint, and judgment falls."[21]

Like Whitefield, there is little reflection on aspects of the social order that must change. Among the vocal, prominent public evangelicals is only the anxiety and paranoia over the collapse of order. But today, like then, there is little thought given to the injustices that permeate the order that various conspiracies threaten to destroy. This gospel framed as a conspiracy-busting operation always turns a blind eye to the injustices perpetuated by so-called order and is forever associating the incursion of chaos from the outside with the urgency and call to repentance.

Early in American history, evangelicals preached a gospel that adapted itself to the conspiratorial anxiety of whites across the colonial South. To these communities, always in perpetual fear of revolts by the subjugated, the gospel of the Great Awakening was a message that promised the pacification of the enslaved as a *part* of Christian salvation.

As American history progresses, we see this willingness to frame the gospel as a conspiracy-busting force, time and time again. The target of these anxieties may change—be it the enslaved or the secretive claims of Illuminati—but the impulse to use the social anxieties to give the gospel message an urgency and a relevancy is a long-standing play in the evangelical playbook.

RECONSTRUCTION

As America expanded, the evangelical totality of holy paranoia evolved along with it. While the social anxieties and conspiratorial narratives of revolts had framed and fueled the evangelical gospel in the pre–Civil War era, America's ascendancy from a provincial to imperial power after the Civil War also marked an evolution of this conspiratorial gospel.

In the aftermath of the Civil War, a new sort of evangelicalism emerged alongside a new America. We won't understand how this evangelical Christianity took shape apart from a period known as Reconstruction.

After the Civil War, the federal government occupied the southern states to ensure the restoration of the Union. The federal government worked to extend the civil rights due the formerly enslaved and legislated a legal pathway back into the Union for the South. Federal troops occupied southern states in order to enforce the expansion of civil rights for the formerly enslaved in the wake of the passage of the Nineteenth Amendment. Confederate veterans (especially leaders) were required to take oaths of loyalty to the Union. Suffice to say, it was a huge undertaking.

The period of Reconstruction is marked by its near constant source of social strain and political violence. In one episode that bears an uncanny resemblance to January 6, 2021, a private militia of Confederate veterans called the Crescent City White League stormed the state capitol in New Orleans to install their candidate for governor in what they claimed was a corrupt election.

They were resisted (oddly enough) by Robert E. Lee's right-hand general, a former Confederate general, James Longstreet, who led an integrated Louisiana state militia of white and Black Americans against the Confederate veterans. It was called the "Battle of Liberty Place" by the old Confederates, who actually succeeded in installing their candidate for a few days before federal troops arrived and eventually displaced them.

A monument to the Battle of Canal Street was erected in New Orleans. But like January 6 today, the monument altered memory. The memorial commemorated not the Battle of Canal Street but the "Battle of Liberty Place," the name used by white supremacists. It stood in New Orleans until 2017, when it was removed under police escort for fear of violent retribution.

The period of Reconstruction is filled with episodes of terror like this. Reconstruction saw the rise of the Ku Klux Klan and with it the spread of vigilante, race-based violence. Disparate lynchings, theft, and beatings erupted across a nation where the armies of North and South had been dispersed, but the hatreds had not been extinguished.

Reconstruction ended "officially" in the presidential election of 1877, when a hung electoral process resulted in backdoor political dealings. The Republican candidate Rutherford B. Hayes would be given the White House in exchange for an end to Reconstruction, including the withdrawal of federal troops from the South. This eliminated the necessary accountability to ensure civil rights, leading to the emergence of Jim Crow laws across America.

But to white Americans, the end of Reconstruction appeared different. The reason many white Americans cannot recall the way Jim Crow laws came to be enacted after a Civil War to end slavery and can't remember episodes like the Battle of Canal Street is because of what's become known as a cult of reconciliation.

In the wake of Reconstruction, whites across the South and North reconciled at the expense of African Americans, who were denied civil rights in the process. The creation of Jim Crow rolled back the civil rights enforced by Reconstruction. For example, during Reconstruction the state of Georgia elected several African Americans, like Henry McNeal Turner and Tunis Campbell, to its state legislature.

When Reconstruction ended, so did the freedoms guaranteed by federal troops. Georgia attempted to expel African Americans in 1868, only to be forced to reseat some, until it finally succeeded in disenfranchising African Americans in 1908. It wasn't until 1962 that an African American, Leroy Johnson, was elected to the state legislature again.

Whites on both sides of the Civil War sought to patch up the wounds of the conflict, but did so by capitulating to segregationist policies and enabling cultural practices of terror.

In the nineteenth century, evangelist D. L. Moody found himself right in the midst of this crucible. A former chaplain to Union soldiers, Moody soon became, in the mold of Whitefield, a global celebrity during the period of Reconstruction.

Though personally opposed to segregation, Moody's revivals became a site of and host to his day's prevailing social conflict, the insidious capture of American society by the powers of white supremacy and Jim Crow. In a report from one of his revival rallies from Augusta, Georgia, in 1876, we find a good example of this capture:

> When he first began holding his open-air meetings here, negroes mingled so indiscriminately with the audience that it became disagreeable to the whites, and a dividing fence was put up. Mr. Moody did not like this, and spoke of it, when one of our pastors informed him that it was impossible for the blacks and whites to mingle even in a religious audience. Mr.

Moody then said, "I see you have not gotten over your rebellious feelings yet." "No," said the minister, "I am proud of my rebellious feelings and will be a rebel until I die." The conversation was designably interrupted by others, and the matter was dropped.[22]

Moody's revival rallies were attended en masse right up to the turn of the twentieth century. And it was only at the end where Moody's personal criticism of segregation had begun to evolve into the courage to act. In the judgment of historian Edward Blum,

> At the height of his public power in the 1870s, Moody had not challenged the racial status quo. He had kept quiet; he had prized unity among whites over human brotherhood. In the years that white Americans flocked to hear him and sat riveted by his stories, he had refused to stand against the tide of racial prejudice and segregation. In fact, he had brought the force of his own spiritual authority to propel those waters. When Moody did raise against segregation in the 1890s, Jim Crow was too firmly entrenched in American society.[23]

During the era of Reconstruction and its collapse under the cult of reconciliation, Moody's ministry gave evangelical Christianity a public, national platform. He founded institutions that exist to this day, such as the Moody Bible Institute in Chicago.

Holy paranoia in the Reconstruction era proved a Christian gloss to the cult of reconciliation. It spoke of divine forgiveness that enabled the perpetuation of injustice. And it triumphed among white evangelicals over the harder task of Reconstruction. At the expense of minority Americans, whites in the North and the South, Union and Confederate, opted to "forgive" one another. But this forgiveness was politically expedient, contingent upon a forgetting that brought about the destruction of civil rights and the creation of Jim Crow America. Conspiratorial suspicions about African Americans did not go away with the Civil War, of course; they evolved. This created a social order permeated by white supremacy and primed for conspiratorial suspicion to be cast against immigrants of all sorts.

A NEW CONTROVERSY

The rise of Moody occurred alongside an academic trend that was soon to fracture whatever unity Moody had secured. In Germany, scholars began to critically engage the biblical texts in a movement known as "high criticism"—which cast doubts on the historical veracity of the texts.

Before the tide of high criticism, the "evangelical" label was at a saturation point in American society. The federal government's census in 1890 listed 90 percent of American Protestants as "evangelicals." But this unity soon fractured, dividing into camps of modernists (those who favored high criticism) and fundamentalists (those who did not).

In the early twentieth century, to be "evangelical" spoke of a bygone era of unity that could never be recovered. You were either a modernist who could reconcile biological evolution with the biblical witness or a fundamentalist who rejected it outright. Both laid claim to the evangelical label. But the holy paranoia we are tracing took on a unique feature in its path through fundamentalism up to our present.

In the Scopes Trial of the 1920s, former presidential candidate William Jennings Bryan railed against the teaching of evolution in public schools. He claimed evolution was an affront to clear biblical teaching, which was the grounds of American education. The fundamentalist view, which Bryan didn't subscribe to wholesale,[24] won at trial, but was later overturned on a legal technicality.

The difference between a modernist and a fundamentalist had to do, largely, not with a view of cosmology, but whether or not one embraced the insights of high German liberal theological scholarship. Moody quickly sided with fundamentalists, rejecting all scholarship that seemed to question some of the basic historically perceived tenets of the Christian faith, including an embrace of evolutionary theory and questioning the historicity of Jesus's resurrection.

Ironically, fundamentalists cast themselves as defenders

of the faith, but did so in a way that sought to prove Christianity by the terms modernism imposed. In other words, if high criticism cast doubt on the "fact" of Noah's ark, then fundamentalists insisted it was indeed a "fact" that could endure the scrutiny of modern scientific standards and methods. This shift among fundamentalists persists today in the clamoring after "fact" as the sum total proof of "faith."

Now, this all may not seem consequential. What, after all, do theological conflicts have to do with conspiracy theory and holy paranoia? The point in recounting all this is that these controversies and periods of change provided the categories and even preemptive conclusions that organized the evangelical mind for generations to come.

And so to this period of change, we need to add one more distinctive characteristic of fundamentalists to set them apart from modernists, and that is the novel end times theology of dispensationalism. Popularized by the likes of John Nelson Darby, C. I. Scofield, and others, dispensationalism is most well-known for advancing the idea of a Rapture where Jesus takes his church up to heaven, leaving non-Christians behind to face a seven-year "tribulation period."

The idea of a Rapture was rooted in a larger claim: dispensationalism held that history itself could be mapped in a very clear, predicable progression. This mapping was revealed by a particular reading of the Bible, a cryptographic way of reading that revealed the code to only the most serious and expert readers.

This "end times" theology, or more properly "eschatology," proved to be a significant power source for charging conspiracy theory as akin to dispensationalism's rigid understanding of what counted as "biblical prophecy."

History became a code, and the Bible, the key. Reading the Scriptures in this sense did more than ascribe meaning to history; it offered certainty and specificity—insight into the unfolding of events themselves.

Every time something unexpected happened, fundamentalists opened the Bible believing that things like the fascist rise of Mussolini were specifically predicted *by* the Bible, and so *proved* the Bible's validity.

Here's why this all matters for holy paranoia. This effort to *prove* the Bible shattered the Bible. By reducing it to a cryptic index of geopolitical prophecies of the end times, the Bible was robbed of its unique authority. In this current, the Bible was transformed into an indexable set of facts and not a witness to a story.

Modern evangelicals today trace their historical lineage through fundamentalists of the early twentieth century, not the modernists. And the political activities of these fundamentalists are instructive not only for the ideological capture of evangelicals today, but also for the way this history shaped and conditioned the theology of evangelicalism.

Significantly, the use of conspiracy theory to buttress and defend fundamentalist theology and its application to geopolitical events, culture, and society all served to further capture fundamentalist evangelicals toward aligning the kingdom of God with the American Empire. This meant that threats to the American Empire were coded as threats to the church as well.

During World War I, which confirmed to many fundamentalists the accuracy of their prophetic calendars, revivalists promoted a white supremacist nationalism folded into Christianity. The evangelical revivalist Billy Sunday preached of immigrants, "They call us the melting pot. Then it's up to us to skim off the slag that won't melt into Americanism and throw it into hell."[25] Patriotic sentiment during the war rose, as did suspicion of all foreign-born Americans.

Fundamentalists traded in these suspicions all the same, finding in this conspiratorial jingoistic fervor an urgency and relevancy to their gospel proclamation.

To them, as historian Matthew Sutton observed, fundamentalism carried the confidence that biblical morality and "clear" readings of the Scriptures would also result in things like, for example, enforcing the color line and preventing women from voting.[26] Put simply, the conspiratorial read of threats to America, whether from the immigrant, the African American, or the feminine, all coalesced into a single conspiratorial front threatening American greatness. And the theology of fundamentalism continued to attach itself to these conspiracies.

And yet still, these social anxieties were felt alongside global "prophetic" events. In the aftermath of World War I, the creation of the League of Nations as a first-of-its-kind international body meant to stave off nationalist aggression and prevent war drew cries of tyranny and seemingly confirmed to the fundamentalists that the prophetic predictions of the Bible were coming true. Of course, this prophetic theology wasn't just concerned with American nationalist ambition, but also the global events. So alongside conspiracies at home, framed in terms of biblical morality, there were also conspiracies of global tyranny that suited the fundamentalist evangelical eschatology.

One of the most notorious conspiracies of the early twentieth century emerged from Russia, in the form of a fraudulent pamphlet called "The Protocols of the Elders of Zion." Published in 1903, it claimed to detail Jewish plans for global dominance. These plans seemed to be confirmed in the wake of the Russian Revolution in 1917, which created the Soviet Union.

In the hands of White Russians, those defeated by the communist "Reds," the protocols were used to associate the communists with Jews. As late as 1938, the protocols were being used in Nazi Germany elementary education.

Back in America, during the 1920s, American industrialist Henry Ford published elements of the protocols in his Dearborn independent newspaper. The *Moody Monthly*, a publication claiming to represent fundamentalists and associated with the institutions and legacy of D. L. Moody, even commented on the protocols' international reception with unflinching support, saying that they "simply gave to its readers what had been well known for some time to the thoughtful people of Great Britain."[27] The national scene was no better.

Emerging in the wake of the Civil War only to decline amid the cult of reconciliation, the tensions of the 1920s had brought about a revival of the Ku Klux Klan. This fact was celebrated by one letter to the editor published by Moody, who celebrated the return of the Klan as an answer to the problem that "for years a silent penetration of our national institutions has been going on. Subtle mischief is at work. Nefarious combinations have grown so powerful as to present a national menace."[28] Conspiratorial suspicion was the driving narrative fuel of fundamentalist theology applied to the world it inhabited.

The fundamentalist theological imagination seemed to confirm not question the common conspiracy theories of their time, even supercharging them. These antisemitic and white supremacist conspiracies fit hand in glove with the moral pronouncements of fundamentalists, like Harold Ockenga, an associate of Billy Graham who used sermons to warn of Jewish propaganda in Hollywood and cast doubt on whether the color line could ever be abolished.[29]

FDR was not only criticized, but his administration was seen to be a harbinger of tyranny and the antichrist. In this climate, evangelicals came to embrace a posture of "anti-state statism" that persists today: highly critical of government intervention while paradoxically reliant upon government subsidies for their institutions and churches.[30] Seemingly from every angle, whether national or international, fundamentalist evangelicals trafficked in the conspiracy theories that characterized America's experience between the wars.

COLD WAR CONSPIRACY

Ten days after the official end of World War II, in August 1945, an American intelligence officer by the name of John Birch was shot and killed by Chinese communist forces. He had grown up in a small fundamentalist Baptist church and had gone to China as a missionary in 1940, before the war.

Growing up, Birch came under the influence of the fundamentalist preaching of J. Frank Norris, whose penchant for dispensationalism found him accusing the Harding administration of committing "national suicide" by its efforts to disarm after World War I.[31] This was a feature, rather than a bug, of fundamentalism.

Because its end times theology perceived empty chaos until the return of Christ, its political solutions fit hand in glove with a decidedly right-wing reactionary ethos and trenchant militarism. This perception hailed the power of the State as the deciding power, while harboring a corresponding suspicion of government as a threat to State exercise.

Birch committed himself to be a missionary to China during one of Norris's sermons. He followed through. But when war broke out between the US and Japan, he found himself in an unlikely position. His ecumenical church contacts throughout China—which was fractured between an occupying Japanese force, Chinese communists to the north, and democratic Chinese to the west—could be harnessed as a vast intelligence network. And so Birch did both. He enlisted, achieving the rank of captain before his death, while also performing ecumenical ministry across China.

But it was a businessman, by the name of Robert Welch, who would introduce America to the story of John Birch. Welch was, like Birch (and me at one point in time), a fundamentalist Baptist. He was a member of the National Association of Manufacturers, whose commitment to free market capitalism made the association a staunch critic of the New Deal and the FDR administration, which fundamentalists often associated with tyranny.

Welch's suspicion and animosity toward communism resonated with the story of John Birch. He called Birch the "first casualty" of the Cold War, and in his book *The Life of John Birch* peddled the conspiracy theory that the US government had covered up the details of his death.[32] In truth, Welch learned of Birch's death through easily accessible government records.

Welch founded the John Birch Society in 1958. It was

immensely popular with white Americans. The reason, in the words of historian Matthew Dallek, had to do with the prevailing conservative position in the postwar moment:

> In the aftermath of depression and world war, the expansion of government control over their lives felt grotesque, a constitutional violation that inalterably sapped the strength of capitalism. Welch's conspiracy theories landed easily too; rather than being alien to the far right's culture, they were endemic to it.[33]

The John Birch Society brought together largely white, middle-class Americans to become what Dallek deemed a "third-party shock force" on American political life.[34] Though it never came to dominate the conservative movement, it succeeded in harassing Supreme Court judges and forcing presidential candidate Barry Goldwater to walk a tightrope, disavowing Welch while courting Birchers.

The JBS was a community constituted at its very core by conspiracy theory. But like QAnon today, it wasn't *just* a theory. It was an entire reality. If QAnon claims deep state entrenchment, then JBS claimed communist infiltration, everywhere and anywhere. Welch made national news (and tarnished the society's PR) claiming that President Eisenhower was a communist. In time, JBS leaders came to believe that desegregation was a communist plot.[35]

Through its tactics and associations, JBS occupied the

"right of the right," but in truth, evangelicalism never disassociated from it. Rather, evangelicalism domesticated itself to these conspiracies, in both the gospel they preached and the institutions they founded.

In a New Year's Eve sermon delivered in 1951, Billy Graham told the residents of Boston that there were over one thousand socialist or socialist-sounding groups in America working to influence the minds of everyday Americans. This conspiracy, according to Graham, could only be busted by revival.

In the 1950s, Graham's gospel was adapted to the conspiratorial communist anxieties across America. He penned a series of articles on the dangers of communism to Christian America for the *American Mercury*. It was a publication known for its strident antisemitism and conspiracism, and also featured Carl McIntire, a more stringent fundamentalist and avowed JBS member. Personal repentance was seen as the antidote to communist collectivism. It also happened to coincide with the tenets of free market capitalism and opposition to segregation. This front of conservative support created wide space for the holy paranoia of the Cold War.

Conspiracy theory was a dominant strain in American life during the Cold War as a feature of anti-communism. In the early fifties, America endured a "Red Scare" led by the efforts of Senator Joseph McCarthy to oust communists from prominent positions in American society and political life. The JBS encouraged its members to take over parent-teacher associations to ward off communist influence, echoing contemporary "woke panics" that sought to oust anti-racists and equality activists more recently.

Billy Graham went on to found a print magazine in 1956, *Christianity Today*, as a flagship institution to define a new sort of evangelical. His primary source of funding came from an oil magnate named J. Howard Pew, a JBS member.[36] The former news editor of *Christianity Today*, Danial Silliman, in an article on the magazine's origins, quotes Pew's motivation for the venture involved

> getting "preachers back to preaching the Bible." . . . [W]hat he meant by this was that ministers would stop criticizing capitalism. "We can never hope to stop this Country's plunge toward totalitarianism," Pew wrote a few years before he started funding *Christianity Today*, "until we have gotten the ministers' thinking straight." Pew believed the clergy were undermining American free markets with unfair and uninformed critiques of business. Ministers, he said in 1960, "were doing more to promote socialism and communism than anyone else." They needed to be reeducated.[37]

Christianity Today is a flashpoint for the way the totality of holy paranoia was reinforced by and evolved through the Cold War. It's not that conspiracy theory was universally upheld by evangelicals, it's more that it was never exorcised for reasons of political and economic expediency. Holy paranoia evolved and persisted.

A good example of this can be found in the January 7, 1966, issue of *Christianity Today*. It featured a back cover advertisement for a new curated mail-order book list called the Conservative Book Club,[38] founded two years earlier in 1964.[39] It offered all subscribers a copy of *The Liberal Establishment* by M. Stanton Evans. In large, bold text, the ad describes Evans's "takedown" of liberalism:

> The Liberals cry out "more for freedom for all!" while they systematically plunder our liberties . . . and leave our darkened streets swarming with admitted criminals![40]

In claiming to expose the dark truths of American society, the Conservative Book Club billed itself as apocalyptic—*revealing* what it claimed to be the actual movers and shakers of its political moment.

This revelation, though, was not just conspiratorial, but also marketing rhetoric, aimed directly at *Christianity Today*'s evangelical audience. Other books for sale traded in some of the same conspiratorial tropes that organized the John Birch Society.

This was an affiliation not lost on readers. Letters poured in to *Christianity Today* accusing the Conservative Book Club of being a front for the Birch Society.[41] These readers demanded to know, was *Christianity Today* endorsing the John Birch Society?

In two subsequent issues, the letters to the editors section hosted a reader's debate.[42] Some questioned why *Christianity Today* promoted far-right politics. One wrote,

> The Conservative Club, as we know in our area, is a front for the John Birch Society, a dangerously extremist organization.[43]

Another reader disagreed in the next issue, stating,

> Even if there were something undesirable about the Conservative Book Club, their advertisement proved only that they and *Christianity Today* are in agreement regarding advertising, not necessarily politics. The ... club isn't "a front for the John Birch Society," as claimed. Being a JBS member, I think I would know if it were.[44]

This reader debate took place over the course of three months in 1966. Such a small historical sample hardly seems notable in and of itself. But it illustrates the way in which this evangelical totality of holy paranoia persists and evolves. The conspiratorial narrations, charged by theology and contained in a leading evangelical publication for advertising profit, show how a nexus of variables can contribute to its spread.

There were also more direct means. *Christianity Today* offered editorial space to FBI Director J. Edgar Hoover. Hoover provided a series of articles both describing the communist worldview and comparing it to the "Christian" worldview. This not only resulted in identifying the national identity of Americans with Christianity, but it also coded anyone who failed to satisfy that criteria as a moral deviant, and a national security threat, a target of state-sanctioned violence.

DEEP-STATE ANTISEMITISM

But it wasn't just communism. As new evangelicals like Graham became politically ascendant, they enjoyed political access, the likes of which fundamentalists decades earlier could only have dreamed. Notably, Billy Graham became a close friend and personal confidant of President Richard Nixon.

Nixon would often record his meetings in the White House, including his conversations with Graham. One conversation that Nixon had with Graham was one where the president expressed his frustration over the way the media was treating him. Recently, *The Washington Post* had published, against the threats of the government, a series of documents that came to be known as the Pentagon Papers.

The papers were damning. They detailed a government cover-up over the true extent of the conflict in Vietnam. In short, the American public had been lied to. (Proof that government secrecy itself can be the source of conspiracy theory.) But this sort of government corruption was not the topic of conversation between Nixon and Graham one day in 1973.

Instead, Nixon began to rail against media figures whom he blamed for his faltering popularity and efficiency. He articulated his frustration through using tired, antisemitic tropes that shared marked similarities with the sort of antisemitic conspiracy theories propagated by the *Protocols* at the turn of the century. "Insofar as the media is concerned, the powerful media, they've [the Jews] got it."[45] The tape registers Graham's agreement.

The Oval Office recordings reveal Graham corroborated Nixon's frustrations with the "Jewish" media by offering him a conspiratorial, antisemitic interpretation of Scripture that reinforced those very tropes. Here is a transcript of the full conversation:

> Graham: "The Bible, Mr. President, makes a distinction between two types of Jews, and one is called the synagogue of Satan. Those people in the latter days will be called the remnant of God's people, which will be Jewish people. And then there's the Synagogue of Satan. And all of your religious deceptions in the latter days [will come from this group] and they are energised by supernatural power called the Devil, and this is what the Bible teaches. Whether or not you believe it, I believe it."

> Graham: "And I believe the Jews have a strange brilliance about them. They're smart. They are energised by a supernatural power. And you see, Hitler . . . they [the Jews] had a stranglehold on the banking of Germany on everything in Germany. But he went about it wrong. But this stranglehold has got to be broken or this country is going to go down the drain."
>
> Nixon: "Do you believe that?"
>
> Graham: "Yes sir."
>
> Nixon: "I can never say it, but I believe it."[46]

We must recognize that the evangelical inheritance of this historical impulse to distrust the "media" has its roots in elements of antisemitism. This doesn't let legacy or new media off the hook; it doesn't code all criticism of the "media" as antisemitic. Rather, struggling with the scandal of evangelical history suggests that the inherited impulse toward suspicion that has traveled across evangelicalism must be examined and dismantled where it traffics in uncritical tropes and reactionary distrust.

LEFT BEHIND

As the twenty-first century came into view, evangelicals became a key part of the base that elected Ronald Reagan to the presidency. Once again, they built grassroots networks, founded political institutions, and—right alongside—the conspiratorial totality evolved, yet again. This time, the usual suspects (women, ethnic and sexual minorities) included secular humanists. One evangelical leader said it plainly:

> I myself have been a forty-five-year student of the satanically-inspired, centuries-old conspiracy to use government, education, and media to destroy every vestige of Christianity within our society and establish a new world order. Having read at least fifty books on the *Illuminati*, I am convinced that it exists and can be blamed for many of man's inhumane actions against his fellow man during the past two hundred years. . . . An enormous amount of evidence proves that secularization of our once Judaeo-Christian society has not been an accident but is the result of the devilishly clever scheming carried on by this secret order.[47]

These words belong to pastor, activist, and coauthor of the Left Behind novel series Tim LaHaye. The series reinforced the totality of holy paranoia for a new generation, even those who were not sitting in evangelical churches.

The success of the novels was so great in the 1990s and 2000s that, looking back, historian Daniel Hummel credits the series with diffusing an apocalyptic cocktail into the cultural mainstream.[48] The books were a dramatic interpretation *and* application of the end times theology contained in dispensationalism.

Beginning with the chaotic rapture in which billions of Christians instantly vanish from the world (causing planes to fall from the sky and cars to veer off the road), readers were introduced to the fictional rise of a totalitarian globalist government through the machinations of the antichrist, a European leader named Nicolae Carpathia.

But the whole point of these books, while fictional, was that they anticipated something that was *definitely* going to happen, according to streams of evangelicalism. The point isn't to lay holy paranoia at the feet of dispensationalism. For the uninitiated, this -ism is a packaged set of beliefs about what the Bible teaches about history and its end. It teaches the idea of a "rapture," where every Christian disappears in an instant and goes to be with Jesus. In the books, that event was always chaotic—with planes falling from the sky presumably because the pilot was a Christian. There was a conspiracy theory popular among evangelical spaces that said American Airlines actually didn't let two Christian pilots fly the same flight to mitigate that risk.

I read the kids' version of the novels growing up. The summary of the kids' novels audiobook began with the following line: "What do you do when your greatest fear becomes reality?"[49] I cannot understate the impact these books and their vision of a totalitarian future had on my concept of devotion to Jesus, and the dread and doubts that came along with it. This maps neatly onto the conspiratorial and the totality of holy paranoia, with its penchant for knowing the "true" meaning behind a political event along with the dread and anxiety that comes with anticipating totalitarian persecution of Christians.

The irony shouldn't be lost on us that a generation of evangelicals were steeped in stories forming an anticipation for the rise of a totalitarian antichrist coupled with the present adulation of MAGA Christianity for Donald Trump.

But the irony is extinguished at a deeper examination. LaHaye's theology was explicitly conspiratorial.

LaHaye's conspiracism is the prototype for the theologically charged conspiracism and suspicion that so dominates our current moment. This isn't to suggest that LaHaye alone is the source, but rather he exemplifies the way in which holy paranoia evolved alongside right-wing political action, giving today's evangelicals their inheritance of holy paranoia.

But how did these theological beliefs go mainstream? It wasn't *only* through the popularity of Christian fiction, but political action, too.

You remember in the first chapter how we told the story of Jerry Falwell and his VHS documentary, *The Clinton Chronicles*, sold on his television program *The Old-Time Gospel Hour*. Taken by itself, it is just one of many examples of conspiratorial politics given a supercharge by its association with evangelical Christianity. But the plausibility for these conspiracies was sourced from the accumulation of political power, too.

Falwell's Moral Majority in the 1980s, which captured the evangelical vote for Ronald Reagan, signaled a massive change in the American electorate. LaHaye, Falwell, Pat Robertson, an entire new "cast" of evangelicals came to the forefront as their politically savvy brand of evangelical sought political power and influence for the first time in a generation.

Let's get back to LaHaye. Not only was he a member of the John Birch Society, he also became the first president of a vast donor network and political coalition cofounded by Reagan Republican strategist Paul Weyrich and Southern Baptist president Paige Patterson.[50] The coalition became known as the Council for National Policy, organized in the wake of the successful Reagan campaign.[51]

Together, the CNP and Reagan administration influenced policy that continues to shape the present. One of the capstones of Reagan's presidency was the rescinding of the Federal Communications Commission's Fairness Doctrine in 1987.[52] Under this standard, media organizations had been required by law to provide a balanced presentation of viewpoints in the presentation of particular opinions. Rush Limbaugh's nationally syndicated radio program began less than a year following the rollback of the Fairness Doctrine.[53]

In the vacuum left by the repeal of the Fairness Doctrine, conservative talk radio exploded in force. Part of this expansion occurred on track laid by evolving evangelical media ecosystems. Older forms of evangelical media like the traditional preaching programs, which had long been associated with fundamentalists and evangelicals alike, consolidated with new media like Christian music *and* conservative talk radio.

The CNP is a concentration of these radio empires, particularly Salem Communications, American Family Radio, and Bott Radio; the founders of all three media groups are CNP members.[54] Salem Media owns a radio and podcasting network with ninety-nine stations that fuses Christian content with conservative politics, and more than half of those stations operate in one of the country's largest twenty-five markets.[55] Evangelical media ecosystems like these make it so that CCM (contemporary Christian music) can be heard alongside Charlie Kirk and Turning Point USA. The association creates a powerful devotion, one that unites *worship* with the *words* of conservative platforms.

CNP AND THE BIG LIE

This devotion was primed by the CNP during the first Trump presidency. Its network flexed its power to prime and then propagate President Trump's claim that the 2020 election was stolen.

The CNP proceedings and member list are normally secret. But this hasn't prevented leaks. Between October 2019 and February 2020, the CNP hosted two gatherings, which together were called 2020 Vision.[56] In the October 2019 gathering, there was a special "Action" panel featuring attorney Sidney Powell. Between the 2020 election and January 6, Powell was part of President Trump's legal team and was eventually sanctioned for her legal practices related to bringing suits alleging election fraud[57] in line with Trump's claims.

The title of Powell's 2019 panel was "How to Stop the Deep State Assault on Our Republic." In the panel, Powell referred frequently to the "deep state."[58] To Powell, the deep state existed solely in opposition to freedom and to Republicans.[59]

Powell went on to narrate a series of legal actions brought against Republicans and business leaders meant to substantiate her claim that conservatives, in the sociopolitical climate, are a "persecuted minority" and potential "political prisoners" subject to an immune prosecutorial Department of Justice.[60] In the years to follow, Trump's rhetoric on "lawfare" and January 6 defendants as "political hostages" capitalized on this base.

But it isn't just internalized deliberations. It is also externalized through media empires. In October 2019, two weeks after the CNP gathering, Charlie Kirk, CNP member and founder of Turning Pointing USA, tweeted to over a million followers, "RT [Retweet] if the Senate should ACT and fight back against Democrats' deep state coup!"[61] One tweet on November 28, 2020, claims, "Voter fraud is real."[62] Another on December 4, 2020, reads, "There is more evidence of systemic voter fraud in America than 'systemic racism,' yet which one do you think Democrats are more worried about?"[63]

Years later, evangelicals are still unable to speak about these events without betraying the still-active holy paranoia that draws us toward willed ignorance, complicit silence, or confusing the ascendancy of Trump back to the presidency as absolution for political falsehoods of expediency.

REMEMBERING WHAT HAS BEEN FORGOTTEN

"Memory," says Stanley Hauerwas, "is a moral exercise."[64] There is no authorized story of evangelical Christians in America, nor can there ever be. But to tell the truth about holy paranoia in the present demands an honest reckoning with it in the past. This is the work not just of historians, but any who are morally awake.

The rise of conspiracy theory that we are experiencing today is inseparable from the history of evangelicalism in America. There is no period of so-called evangelical history when a segment of evangelicals is not trafficking in conspiracy theory. And this trafficking in the paranoid always advances or relies on some sort of theological claim. Whether

Whitefield's contention that God used slavery to bring the gospel to Africans, or LaHaye's that the Illuminati were organizing to disrupt Christian influence on American politics. These conspiracy theories are always referred to the world of evangelical theology. In this hermetically sealed world, they're given a theological charge that makes them impervious to "fact-checking." This is totality at work, a strategy that is fundamentally a storytelling act.

While the use of conspiracy theory varies, whether directing political action or coding social relationships, evangelicals have been quick to take the content that conspiracy theory generates and set it inside their own theological imagination.

That being said, we've seen how conspiracy theories don't often originate with evangelicals themselves. They emerge from the anxieties and identities that are latent in the American experiment. Whether maintaining the institution of slavery, or the creation of Jim Crow in the wake of reconciling northern and southern whites, or fears over immigrants and communist infiltration, or claims of a pervasive deep state, these suspicions are not unique to Christians. As Americans, evangelicals have their own theologically charged reception of these narratives.

Conspiracism erupts from the social order of America in an attempt to preserve that so-called "order" by telling stories in service of that order. Pushed further, holy paranoia seizes these stories and transforms them from claims of fact to content for a confession of faith. This isn't formal, but informal. You won't find it included in statements of faith on church websites, but you'll hear it in whispers of why someone is "in" or "out." This is how conspiracism comes to signal a *theological* crisis—a crisis of faith. When claims of a stolen election run adjacent to whether or not you're a faithful Christian, facts *and* faith are implicated.

Conspiracy theories retain their usefulness to evangelicals precisely because they offer content that props up and legitimizes the totalizing story evangelical Christians in America trust and offer a witness to.

As these historical episodes show, the totality at the heart of evangelicalism isn't just the Christian story, is it? It contains a story, a myth, of America. Evangelicals have made use of conspiracy across their history to promote their politics, to give urgency and relevancy to their perception of the gospel, and, most essentially, to preserve the totality that stands in for "reality." To find our way forward, we must break this totality down to its most essential elements, performing an autopsy that will lead us on the way of apostasy, out and away from holy paranoia.

Chapter 4

THE PLOT DEVICES OF HOLY PARANOIA

> **Because truth is not trusted, specious propaganda takes over. Because justice is not trusted, whatever is useful is declared to be just.**
>
> —Dietrich Bonhoeffer

I had left my church in Virginia a few months before January 6, 2021. But I hadn't yet left the country. I had accepted a position in a PhD program in Aberdeen, Scotland. And I was busy packing and attending to last-minute travel details that day.

Like most people, I followed the chaos on socials. I

couldn't look away—not just by the scandal of it all, but the symbols. All from my childhood, flashing across the screen. There was the Christian flag—a constant fixture on the church stage from my childhood—right next to the Confederate battle flag. Signs invoking the name of Jesus. Crosses. I knew I wasn't just watching an attempted insurrection. I was watching terror as worship.

Given my proximity to DC, it felt like a local event—because it was. In the weeks that followed, I learned a local partisan group used my former church's parking lot as their meet-up point for January 6.[1] Whether they granted permission, I'll never know. But the blurred lines persist.

In the years since, the memories of January 6 have given way to myths. Now, to be a participant in January 6 is something that earns you speaking invitations. Mass pardons have not so much created myths as they've *continued* the myth that fueled the day to begin with. In spite of all facts to the contrary, facts of court proceedings and lack of evidence, the claim that the election was stolen retains its power and force. This is the power of storytelling, too—it activates the weaponization of forgetting.

The stories that bind MAGA together, that trade on elements of evangelical faith, have a displacing power, too. By dictating their own reality, this totality sets itself up as the unquestionable truth. No other view is possible, no light gets in. Even now, to talk about January 6 among evangelicals tends to duplicate the same framing that exists in the whole of America—insurrection or tourist group? Fascists or patriots?

The totality ignores that it was prayer that made January 6 possible. Any interpretation of that day that doesn't include and involve the priming influence of disoriented Christian devotion will be shallow and misleading.

Several evangelical leaders performed the priming themselves:

Franklin Graham, son of Billy Graham, posted:

> Join me in praying that if there is fraud, it would be proven—for the good of our nation & all future elections. Forces of evil are at work, & we know how much is at stake. Pray for God's will to be done in the outcome of this important election.[2]

Eric Metaxas, evangelical author and podcaster, posted:

> Those criticizing the Jericho March gathering in DC are straining at a gnat to swallow a camel. Where is the outrage at those who would dare to steal an election? Where is the call for transparency & investigation? Those of us gathered were there to pray that God would intervene.[3]

Tony Perkins, President of the Family Research Council, posted:

> Join us as we pray for election integrity in Georgia and that Georgians will elect candidates to the U.S. Senate who will uphold the sanctity of all human life and protect our nation's fundamental freedoms.[4]

Rev. Paula White-Cain, Trump's appointee to the Faith Office, posted:

> I ask you to pray fervently, without ceasing for our nation and the election results. There is great concern that some are trying to steal this election. Let us pray to God, who knows all, to reveal truth. Pray that the enemies to God are quieted and their plans are overturned.[5]

These prayers are a window into a disoriented totality. The last chapter traced the evolution and variations of this totality, how it brought together preaching to pacify white fears of revolts, how it lashed out at immigrants and promised to provide the morality necessary to serve as a conspiracy-busting force against communism.

You can see here how these calls to action, performed as prayer on January 6, are irreducibly Christian. You may have encountered this totality in your church, in your community, or online.

This totality of holy paranoia calcifies the Christian story—it turns it from a living witness that confronts into a static ideology that can only ever confirm and justify those who claim it. If the last chapter surveyed the history of this totality, this chapter examines its individual parts.

It can be helpful to think of each part of this evangelical totality as a plot device. Caught between the story of Jesus and the myths of America, these plot devices come together to create a totalizing perception of the world, a bespoke reality that, in its totality, cannot be questioned. It is certainly more than the sum total of its parts. But each part paves a different pathway to resistance.

APOCALYPSE

Christianity and conspiracy are treated as compatible versions of an apocalyptic story, a story that *reveals* something. We tend to think of "apocalyptic" and "dystopia" as one and the same. But in its most literal sense, apocalypse simply means "to unveil."

As an apocalyptic story, the totality of holy paranoia creates a conspiratorial gospel. If the Christian story *reveals* Jesus as the center and sustainer of the world, the conspiratorial gospel draws from that center to advance its own disorienting revelations, be they about immigrants or sexual minorities or non-citizens—all framed as "biblical" and "enemies of the State." The conspiratorial gospel apocalypses those who threaten to plunge the world into doomsday.

In truth, evangelicalism treats the resurrection of Jesus as the prime alternative fact. Rendered this way, Christian confession serves as a plausibility mechanism for all sorts of alternative knowledge, from vaccines to geopolitics.

But the apocalyptic story that Christianity rehearses *isn't* about the end of the world. When Christians talk about the end of the world, we are really talking about the world's beginning in Jesus. He inaugurates a new Creation characterized by the Hebrew vision of peace called *shalom*—the truthful presence of justice that provides human flourishing for all. But because of the totality of holy paranoia, many read the apocalyptic genres of Scripture and conclude that their Christianity and conspiracy are compatible. They perceive Christianity as offering some sort of escape from a world Jesus abandons and will return to destroy, rather than a life that takes shape in the here and now that anticipates the there and then of Jesus's liberation and rescue.

Ours is a time where the central claim of Christianity is pressed into the service of propaganda and conspiracism. This is because while the claim of resurrection cuts against the grain of what is received as normal and natural, Christian knowledge is taken to be *anything* and *everything* that dissents from "the facts" as presented by non-Christians. There is no common world possible here with such blatant dismissal of fact. There is only the antagonism of Christian versus non-Christian.

Casting the resurrection as the prime alternative fact

expands the apocalyptic quality of the Christian story. When this happens, the risen Jesus comes to authorize *other* transgressive claims or minority reports on things like vaccines, climate change, or the age of the Earth. This totality of holy paranoia operates as a rampant, disoriented apocalypticism. It's been called "end times fascism."[6]

But the resurrection of Jesus isn't the prime alternative fact. Christians do not possess this fact for ourselves. Christians can only confess it. We can only recognize its claim *on us* and find ourselves changed as a result. It is not some rational guarantee that Christians alone are "in the know" or can see into the "room where it happens." When evangelical Christianity in America is characterized by this apocalyptic disorientation, it finds itself in perpetual theological crisis with consequences for the common world.

Dimensions of End Times Fascism

This apocalyptic element has two dimensions. Let's call them "the end" and "the edge," representing two boundaries of human knowledge. The end speaks to the human curiosity about the end of time, of the future with its possibilities of utopia or dystopia. The edge speaks to the human drive to go beyond what we've known or where we've gone before.

But the simple fact that these limits exist doesn't extinguish the allure of transcending human being and its limits. Pride wants to go beyond and get behind. At scale, this is the stuff of Empire—of absolute power, of laying claim to history and occupying every spit of land. But adjusted for the scale of our personal lives, this claim is precisely what conspiracy theory offers. And it can destroy relationships.

In preparing to write this book, I heard from someone who described the pain and loss of her relationship with her dad. Over a period of a few years, she recounted how her dad became increasingly attached to his computer, to Glenn Beck and Rush Limbaugh, and to a variety of counternarratives that, each in their own way, had the transgressive apocalyptic quality—"Here is something *they* don't want *you* to know." The distance and strain on their relationship was matched and measured by the depth of his interest in these alternative narratives. This satisfying sense of being an insider of an outsider group harkens back to that ancient diverging Christianity of Gnosticism and its love for secret knowledge.

I'm often asked if I have a favorite conspiracy theory—an admittedly odd framing, but if I were to play along, I'd say one of my personal favorites is an ancient one, a Roman conspiracy theory known as the Nero Redivivus legend. This legend of ancient Rome best encapsulates the apocalyptic element of holy paranoia and its dimensions of time and space. No better example exists, that I can think of, that illustrates both the pretensions of Empire *and* the personal allure in knowing the end and occupying the edges.

Nero reigned as emperor in the late first century CE, and his unpredictable paranoia and rage resulted in his murdering his second wife and their unborn son. Her memory caused him such guilt that, when he came across an enslaved young boy who was said to resemble her, Nero had him castrated and took him as his wife. The boy took his own life months later. Nero's penchant for debauchery was matched only by his practice of tyranny. He scapegoated Christians as the source of a fire that destroyed a great deal of Rome. He rounded Christians up and burned them alive on stakes around Rome. Conveniently, Nero used the vacant wasteland from the fire to construct his own new palace.

Even with the debauchery and tyranny, Nero's commitment to public works and entertainment earned him popularity with no small part of the Roman people. When he died by suicide, elites welcomed the change. But among those who were partial to Nero, a legend was born: *Nero would return*.

The legend itself shows up in the biblical canon, a fact that owes to the popularity of the narrative itself some thirty-odd years after Nero's demise. In Revelation 13, the writer of John's apocalypse alludes to a beast with a mortal wound to the head (Nero is said to have killed himself with a sword to the neck), but that the beast survived. Whether or not this refers directly to Nero is obviously up for debate. But when we acknowledge how the book of Revelation was meant to disrupt the propaganda that organized Roman power in the late first century Mediterranean, it isn't a stretch.

Centuries later, the Nero Redivivus legend was still around, more potent than ever. But the empire itself had changed. Under Emperor Constantine, the empire had been Christianized. Christians who had once been the scapegoats for Nero's great fire were now privileged, the Roman elite class would converge with Christian bishops over the next five hundred years. In the midst of these alterations in Roman religion, the Roman Empire itself was under siege from incursions by unconquered peoples. It was a situation that led many Romans to surmise that, like Nero, the Christians were to blame. But a bishop from Hippo took issue with this view, and took up a pen. That bishop was St. Augustine. And his response to that criticism, *The City of God*, references the persistent Nero Redivivus legend.

By Augustine's day, the return of Nero had, for many Christians, come to give shape to their understanding of the "anti-Christ." That is, many Christians believed that the resurrection and return of Nero was the coming of the anti-Christ. Augustine wrote then, "I am amazed at the great audacity of those who hold such opinions."[7]

But the Nero Redivivus legend persists up to the present. The legend held that Nero would return "from the East"—the farthest reaches of the empire—to march on the city of Rome and bring about the final, decisive battle for human history. It's a story that should seem familiar to us, even now.

Edge of the World—Unknown Places

Our world has changed. To the ancients, we are gods. On any smartphone, we can gaze down on the Earth at nearly every point. There is no more "edge" of the world as a physical "beyond" occupied by monsters. Satellite imaging has taken away much of the "mystery" of unknown places. But even so, the "unknown" persists in our social networks, our politics, and our economies.

The common story element in most conspiracy theories is a glimpse "beyond the edge" of what is known. Whether it's geopolitics, pandemics, or partisan culture war, conspiracy theory always steps into the fray claiming to divulge and reveal the "truth" that has previously been hidden. This penchant for hidden, transgressive knowledge is precisely what the Nero Redivivus legend provided for ancient Romans and Christians in the West.

The storytelling of conspiracy theory today is no different. Conspiracy theories by and large claim to divulge hidden and transgressive knowledge. What's more is that *awareness* of this knowledge constitutes *conversion*. There's something deeply, fundamentally Christian about this, which we'll return to later.

For now, I just want to emphasize how this holy paranoia totality hosts stories that, like the legend of Nero, attempt to narrate events, actions, and individuals from a perspective *beyond* the boundaries of accepted or assented knowledge. This secret knowledge from beyond the known edge makes them *attractive*. This is why conspiracy theory gives its adherents a sense of supremacy: "I know, you don't." And it's also why conspiracy theory builds community: "I know and *we* know."

End of the World—Unknown Times

Conspiracism also tells a story that narrates how history and the world might end. This doesn't always have to be *the* end, as in of all humanity or the planet. Though this is often the case in Christian receptions of conspiracy theory. Those who grew up consuming the cocktail of apocalyptic fiction like *Left Behind* inside the persecution complex understand how conspiracy theories that claim to explain geopolitical events are always defended by associating them with a particular sort of Christian eschatology (or theology on the culmination of God's work).

Theologians are not unaware of this penchant. It's just that much good theology has not found its way into popular and common spaces. Instead, we have a generation of people who identify as Christians in America who, with a shrug of the shoulders and a slogan "the end times!" can find plausibility for any story that claims to involve the end of the world, be it under the influence of George Soros or another apparent anti-Christ.

But the "end of the world" element of this totality can *also* mean, more practically, that conspiracism tells a story that implies a terminal event: something that changes everything. Nero's marching on Rome was supposed to change everything for the beleaguered Empire. In the same way, the "Coming Storm" of QAnon was supposed to change everything for the swamp of the American Empire. This sense of an imminent, terminal event gives conspiracism immense potency. After all, who doesn't want wrongs to be made right, right away?

There's a moral element animating this urgency. Because for all the data science that exists to articulate the health, quality, and integrity of information, I want to drive home how conspiracy theory thrives as a myth, as a story, with the power to provide hope and shape moral imagination. And this can work in the positive, or the negative.

Take the white anxiety of revolts against the economic system of chattel slavery in the American South. The "end times" event sustained by these conspiratorial stories—an uprising of enslaved people—was something white American slave owners tried to *arrest* and did so through preaching a domesticating gospel. On the other hand, on January 6, the conspiracy of a stolen election implied a terminal event that the insurrectionary mob was mobilized to *hasten*, the disruption of democratic process and the installation of Donald Trump as the 45th president for a second term.

These two elements, the edge of knowledge and end of the world, are present in nearly every sort of conspiracy theory we may come across. We might understand them as the primary plot devices of the conspiratorial totality. This is especially true in Christian spaces where conspiratorial claims become part and parcel to the whole package of "Christian knowledge" under the banner of a "biblical worldview." This worldview goes beyond claiming superiority when confronted with facts by non-Christians, it is totalizing in its silencing of dissent.

And since this book has mainly concerned itself with conspiracy theory as a storytelling act, I want to emphasize the power of the apocalyptic in reinforcing this totality. Christians who claim to possess hidden or superior knowledge from "beyond the borders" of possible knowledge, whose motivation is to either realize or resist some sort of terminal event, are exhibiting a corrosive, faithless suspicion.

Why? Because Christianity isn't secret knowledge; it is an open claim, one that has taken itself public from the very beginning. Like John wrote to the earliest Christians on the margins of the Roman world and their own Jewish community: "What we have seen and heard, we declare to you . . ." (1 John 1:3). To say "I believe" may well be an act of faith. But it isn't meant to be done in secret. And it certainly doesn't grant the epistemological high ground. But this is just what is assumed when Christians participate in and sanction movements of political conquest through human action or coercion on the disoriented claim that Christians should rule.

Jesus himself never took this path. He said as much during questioning by the Roman governor Pilate: "If my kingdom were of this world, my followers would be fighting"

(John 18). This kingdom isn't something for Christians to realize in political action as much as its presence in history is a given *reality*, one we do not possess or own, only reflect and receive.

Christians are more authentically Christian when we talk not about the end of history, but its renewal. Christians are people of the end *because a new beginning has been made* and the church is called into the hope of a future defined by peace and restoration. "The Christian life is a life at the end of time," wrote theologian Jacques Ellul.[8] We are not those whose words and works are to be portents of doom or wielding the power of dominion. Rather, Christians are witnesses to a finished work, for all who confess Jesus is God, and that finished work is the future of all that is broken, made new, and all that is ruined, renewed. The language of Israel's prophets offers the richest imagery for this vision: the wolf lying down with the lamb, both led by a small child.[9] This isn't the imagery of violent imperialism, but radical, unconventional peace and wholeness, again, what the Hebrew Scriptures call *shalom*. The world in which *this* image is possible is promised in the story of the Scriptures—a world of safety, peace, and justice. This vision of a renewed world entirely at peace with itself is betrayed whenever its witness opts for coercion, violence, and oppression.

Witness to this world made new grows comfortable with *not knowing* even as it is confident of the world that is on its way. How does it show this confidence? The credibility of Christian faith has never been established by Christians claiming omniscience and superior knowledge. The credibility of Christian faith always emerges from the mystery of our initiation to the life of Christ and the expression of that life through radical generosity and justice. The way Christians narrate the world around them ought to reflect this life.

WHITE-KNUCKLING INDIVIDUALISM

Individualism is another essential plot device in the totality of holy paranoia. When it comes to individualism, evangelicalism in America is decidedly *of* America. To understand how this comes into play, we need to trace some history that gets us back to the present.

It's helpful to start with Copernicus, the man who initiated a revolution in his own time. When the late Polish astronomer theorized that our planet was *not* in fact the center of the universe—that it was in constant motion *around* the sun—he unsettled and upended how people of his time thought about the world, and our place in it.

And Copernicus wasn't alone. The revolution initiated by the discovery of Earth's revolutions amounted to a transformation of knowledge itself. In the wake of Copernicus, a meticulously mechanical account of the cosmos was not just embraced, but assumed.

God was pushed to the periphery. This was a veiled God,

a divine watchmaker, one at work *behind* natural processes, behind a world that was mechanical and predictable. This was the god of the deists. The god of "providence" invoked in the Declaration of Independence, and the god trotted out today by Christian nationalists to "prove" America was founded as a Christian nation. This is not the God of Israel revealed in the Scriptures.

The Copernican Revolution became the seedbed for modern individualism. Filtered through thinkers like Kant, Nietzsche, and Camus, especially in the West, we have come to think of ourselves *first* as individuals—autonomous and self-actualizing.

Individualism intersects with conspiracy theory by offering a framework for causality, or how one thing leads to another. An individualism that arises from accounts of a mechanical universe follows a direct line of cause and effect. It isn't complex, it isn't chaotic, it is certain. And so it is predictable. But this individualism fails to account for and describe how social worlds actually work.

This sort of individualism shows up in conspiracy theories that argue, for example, that a mass global pandemic was the result of one person's master plan—be it Bill Gates, Joe Biden, or Donald Trump. There's always a mastermind whose plans are carried out to perfection. Once you understand how this individualism sees and so interprets the world, you can't unsee it.

Historian Timothy Melley argues that in postwar America, as mass society emerged, conspiracy theory in American life served a purpose, one in which an "individualist culture conserves its individualism by continually imagining it to be in imminent peril."[10] In other words, conspiracy theory is perhaps so popular in America because of the deep-running current of individualism (and the concept of "freedom" it imagines) that has defined the American experiment.

Evangelicalism, as a participant in the American experiment, isn't exempt. Consider that, at the very same time American mass-society was taking shape in the postwar years, evangelicalism was experiencing a resurgent public presence through Billy Graham, who preached that mass individual conversion would restore American greatness, which meant—among other things—the preservation of capitalism and militarism.

While the message of the gospel has a *personal* dimension, it isn't *determined* by individualism. The great theologian Jürgen Moltmann spelled this out most clearly when he argued at Duke in 1968 that "we always start with the belief that he is 'my' savior and come to age in belief that he is 'the' savior."[11] But many evangelicals treat the personal elements of faith in an individualistic way, priming evangelical faith in America for conspiracy theory.

Conspiracy theory understands the world through a very limited, individualistic account of causality. Things happen, it claims, because *people* and *powerful players* decide they are to happen. But this sort of direct cause/effect does not account for the complexity and chaos of our time. Conspiracy theory falls short not just because of its reliance on questionable information, but also because—as stories—they are too simplistic. They offer caricatures of evil, rather than the sort of banal complexity recognized in the work of Hannah Arendt.

ANSWERING INDIVIDUALISM WITH SOLIDARITY

Howard Thurman, mentor to Martin Luther King Jr., wrote on the Church's trend to fascism in America in 1946. He observed, "The bitter truth is that the Church has permitted the various hate-inspired groups in our common life to establish squatter's rights in the minds of believers because there has been no adequate teaching of the meaning of the faith in terms of human dignity and human worth."[12]

I remember pastoring in New Orleans when, one day, a woman entered our storefront church. She was a mother, and she began telling her story. She hadn't seen her child in twenty years. Her child was a trans woman, and when she announced her transition, the mother's church counseled her that the "biblical" option was to cut off her child. She listened.

For two decades, she had not once spoken to her child. With tears in her eyes, she asked me if it would be OK if she reached out, or even went to LA, where she lived. I simply shared with her that every mother has God's blessing to visit her children.

Looking back, I believe I saw in that concrete moment God's abiding love for all people. But I also encountered, in the moment of decision, the myriad ways in which the church often squelches that love, as Thurman recognized.

One of the most pervasive theological corruptions of individualism is how it encourages a Christianity that confidently discriminates between the saved and the damned. Christians do not get to draw the line of separation, ever. The ease with which conspiracy theory categorizes one group as "good" or "saved" and another as damned (projected onto all sorts of categories of difference, whether they be ethnicity, partisan commitment, or other) reflects a Manichean imagination,[13] not a Christian one.

This stark, individualistic "saved" versus "damned" binary appears all over digital space, adjacent to the conspiratorial talk of immigrant "invasions." For example, I came across a meme on social media shared by an evangelical Trump supporter who used to attend a church I pastored. It read, "The entire U.S. Constitution was written for AMERICANS ONLY. It's NOT The World Constitution, it's the U.S. Constitution. Non-citizens and criminals do not possess rights under this document." The inability to recognize human beings beyond the confines of a nation-state is rooted in a theology that grants Christians the power to adjudicate who is in and who is out.

The theology that sanctions this element of holy paranoia must be met by better theology. Such theology paves a way forward toward a vision of God who stands with the oppressed in an age of resurgent ethno-nationalisms coupled with mass migrations, where millions seek refuge from violence and catastrophe.

Such theology recognizes political citizenship does not start from within the nation. It starts in the recognition of a common humanity that transcends our political orders—because it precedes it. The Christian story provokes this sort of recognition by drawing our attention to God's concern for orphans in adoption, to those whose "belonging" is at risk on the margins of community.

The act of adoption has, for too long, been reduced in Christian circles to an economic transaction and charitable service rendered by parents for children.[14] In Christian theology, adoption speaks to God's welcome and humanity's belonging. "He has predestined us for adoption in Jesus," wrote Paul to ancient Christians in Ephesus.[15] Adoption as God's welcome for humanity is where a Christian understanding of citizenship is located, not the nation or its arbitrary borders. Hans Ulrich puts it this way: "In the biblical tradition orphans are understood as a reminder that every human being belongs a priori to a community constituted by rights and maintained by justice."[16]

This alteration introduced *by* theology *against* theology

throws a wrench in the conspiratorial narratives baked into evangelical ways of being Christian in America today. Theology offers all of us a way back from the white-knuckling individualism with its obsession on "personal rights" toward a more thoroughgoing humanism, one that is theologically grounded in God's becoming human, and the way this welcome reveals our common humanity.

WEAPONIZED MORALITY

Every conspiracy, particularly those that find a home and harbor in evangelical circles, contains a moral dimension. The stories they tell are apocalyptic and moral: "This evil thing is happening," claims the conspiracy. And on the back end of that claim is an implication: good individuals must do something.

The rioters who stormed the Capitol on January 6 did so believing they were in the pursuit of righteousness. And that story has largely taken hold in the minds of many Americans to this day.

This moral dimension is so simple, so obvious, that perhaps it doesn't even register. We move to correct fact first and forget that the pull of conspiracism exerts great force on those for whom the desire to *be* good and *do* good are driving factors.

For all the culture warring of MAGA Christianity, there isn't enough discrimination between (and discernment concerning) the moralities on offer in our moment. There are partisan moralities, that which is good by the party. There are social moralities, that which is good by what is necessary to keep a social order. None of these are the same as a "Christian ethic"—which can never be reduced to a static set of principles.

Sociologist and lay theologian Jacques Ellul helped me differentiate between the Christian ethos and what he calls "social morality." What is social morality? It is the scheme of right and wrong that enables society to keep on being society. Ellul is right: "Morality exists everywhere, in every society, but it isn't necessarily the same."[17] What has happened, to put it simply, is that the social morality of America has been confused with a Christian ethos.

But then the scandal of the Christian faith and its ethos comes in and announces the knowledge of good and evil is off-limits to his creatures. There are no values or principles, "Christian" or otherwise.[18] There is only the waiting on and hearing of God's command.

Because Christians are, or should be, always ready to hear the voice and vision of a God who lives. In other words, our understanding and ethics are meant to be informed by divine relationship, and that means it is our call and responsibility to stay tuned in, listening, and discerning. This means Christians don't get to adopt the slogan "Pro-Life, Pro-God, Pro-Gun"—as if these were self-evident Christian values. This moral vision is subject to the God who alone draws the line between good and evil.

This isn't moral relativism, which often reduces itself to a crass pragmatism, the kind that conspiracy theory at its core ultimately practices. This is a Christian posture that refuses to possess the knowledge of good and evil for ourselves. And conspiracy theory tends to offer just this sort of knowing.

Christian ethicist Brian Brock puts it well: "Much damage has been done by modern Christians when they have assumed that we can act well in every situation if we have in hand a set of moral principles or actions we believe is sufficient for anything that might come our way."[19]

The conspiratorial thinking within evangelicalism trades on this disoriented moral zeal. This assumptive claim to wield "Christian values" as the clear product of God's command has introduced so much chaos into this moment of Disreality, where claims over what is "biblical" construct entire moral schemes and systems that function as a totalizing knowledge of good and evil—something evangelicalism claims to possess for itself, rather than pursue in communion with God.

Evangelicals place so much stock in the literal Garden of Eden or six days of creation while ignoring one of the most forceful teachings of the Creation story: that humanity's seizure of the knowledge of good and evil resulted in the catastrophic entrance of sin, death, and evil into the cosmos. Possession of ultimate knowledge, in other words, was the motivating factor in what evangelicals consider "the fall." This should mean more to them than it does.

By promising to offer *Christian* morality to America,

evangelicals conceive of themselves as the community who alone possess moral knowledge. The seeds for moral justification and authority are ready to sprout in such soil. Conspiracy theories in their moral dimensions fit hand in glove with the sort of moral zeal that occupies evangelicals. There, in the context of conservative evangelicalism, the idea of "objective morals" rooted in "absolute truth" makes it so that all moral questions and ethical reflections are bound up in a zero-sum game of right and wrong. Especially when good and evil end up being rooted in concepts of "natural order." Which *sounds* objective. Until you realize that a century ago, what was then called "natural order" included the subservience of black bodies to white bodies and eugenics, the supremacy of the "master race."

The moral imagination of evangelicalism is caught between a systematized seizure of the knowledge of good and evil or reducing ethical deliberation to a matter of technique and management. Together, this myopic moral imagination trades on certainty while giving plausibility to the moral visions projected by conspiracy theory on whatever social or political event is captivating the zeitgeist.

These systems come to us inside evangelicalism under the authority of adjectives like "biblical" or "Judeo-Christian." Evangelicals are not prepared to question the content of these moral systems, only to embrace them. And so this morality becomes primed for use in propaganda. A great example of this is a Pentagon official justifying the development and deployment of AI technology in the Department of Defense by simple fiat: "We follow Judeo-Christian values."[20]

I share this as an illustration of the way morality is perceived as a sealed, finished conversation. The only task, then, is being able to read the Bible to understand these principles and apply them.

There's so much more than can be said here. But we've said what needs to be said about the way morality frames and supercharges holy paranoia. To the extent evangelicalism continues to understand itself as the *possessor* of the knowledge of what is "natural" and therefore "moral," to that extent it is enclosed by a moral totality that makes use of conspiratorial theories that "play" in the same moral key.

The more conspiracy theories cast the "usual suspects" as the source of evil, be they LGBTQ+ people or non-Christians or Democrats, the more they align with the general moral imagination and perception that already organizes evangelicalism to a greater degree. Conspiracism provides a shortcut from moral deliberation that trades on moral zeal.

ANSWERING MORAL ZEAL WITH HUMILITY

The Christian life is a life-for-others offered to God. It is a *free* life, one open and hospitable to each and every person we encounter, and who encounter us in turn. This sort of offering cannot be manufactured; it is the "living sacrifice" Paul writes of in Romans 12:1–2—a life given for the good of fellow human beings, a life offered to God.

Contrary to the stories conspiracy theory tells and the moral universe they occupy, the Bible does not construct a moral system filled with moral principles that individuals can extract and wield for their own uses and political causes. The Scriptures establish the grounds within which the people of God discern his commands and creatively live in a way that enacts God's mercy in and for the common world.

The way to disrupt holy paranoia within evangelical and broadly Christian spaces is by insisting again and again on moral humility and the worship that issues in witness. Theologian Hans Ulrich recognizes worship as the ground where this Christian ethos both develops and is made clear.[21]

By worship, I do not mean a song set or livestreams on Sunday morning. I mean participation in a community that enacts in and among its members a rehearsal of God's story—a story ultimately about liberating renewal. In the Scriptures, Peter depicts this rehearsal as becoming "partakers of Christ's sufferings"—a way of being in the world that can't be conceived as anything less or anything short of taking up our Crosses, as Jesus taught.[22]

This worship, more "way of life" than manufactured moment, is where Christians come to recognize the ground of the Christian ethos for today. Worship isn't the digging of culture war trenches. Christian ethics isn't a power to be possessed, to be willed and wielded and weaponized as a code. It is a way of Spirit-reliant living that is dynamic, never static—an overflowing love in community for the good of others, all as a testimony to the mercy of God for all people.

FREEDOM

To the founding fathers, the perception that King George III was directing a conspiracy against the colonists and their economic interests legitimized their declaration of independence. And so America has run on conspiratorial fuel ever since, so it's said. And on the surface, there's something to be said for all this. Freedom is a plot device with great potency in the totality of holy paranoia.

Let's go back to the moral slogan "Pro-Life, Pro-God, Pro-Gun." It's a common sight on shirts and bumper stickers across America. It isn't just a slogan, it signals a lifestyle, something consumed just as much as confessed. Ownership of firearms and advocacy for the unborn are styled here as synonyms, both signs of "American freedom" at its supposed best, though many will note the obvious dissonances. Citizens of other countries see this plainly.

Conspiracy theories and propaganda about immigrant invasions, or gun control or vaccines, all of these work to cast any sort of policy solutions and political intervention as undermining freedom, something equated, once again, with what it means to be "Christian."

This of course carries with it a deep sense of "religious" freedom, which I put in quotes simply due to the fact that it tends to speak the loudest of *Christian* freedom in ways that end up diminishing the rights and voices of other expressions of faith, or none at all. The Trump administration's announcement of an "anti-Christian bias" task force should serve as a sufficient example.

This overt, totalizing obsession with American "freedom" and its association with Christianity makes it difficult to consider, let alone admit, how authoritarianism might ever take root. But we know better, now. By casting itself as the purveyor and defender of this freedom, authoritarianism becomes the *desired* political means to accomplish these ends.

In his record of late fascism, the scholar Alberto Toscano goes so far as to name an important paradox that is worth considering here: fascist freedom. For Toscano, fascist freedom is a "blurring" of two competing but ultimately complementary visions of freedom. He writes that fascist freedom

> is sustained by the blurring of the borders between liberal conceptions of freedom and individualism (as market freedom, freedom to own, freedom from interference with individual sovereignty) and what we could term fascist visions of freedom (freedom to

dominate, to rule)—both drawn to aggressive imaginaries of competition or "fitness" and a repulsion for solidarity, care, vulnerability.[23]

Fascist freedom is reflected in many of the dominant conspiracy theories. By their very nature, conspiratorial narratives frequently curate anxiety and draw attention to purported tyrannical attempts to limit freedom, only to reactively trade away freedom in the process.

Fascist freedom also plays as a common theme when introducing disinformation. Disinformation couched in agreement with a nefarious "they" is always more palatable. The notion that one is on the receiving end of information "they" are opposed to grants it a reflexive plausibility. It doesn't have to be an entire conspiratorial narrative. It only needs to be tagged as "something they don't want you to know." And suddenly the idea that seizing on this bit of transgressive knowledge is an expression of "freedom"—well that is a powerful association.

Where does this fascist freedom find theological ground? In an evangelical theology of dominionism. Contrary to the doom and dystopia of dispensationalism, dominionist theology says something else about the future. Rather than imagine history as a state of exception that waits for Jesus's return to make everything right, dominionist theology imagines a triumphant, politically ascendant church. It interprets history as the stage for Christian dominion.

The theological contours of fascist freedom in the totality of holy paranoia are found right here. It doesn't matter that dominionism and dispensationalism cultivate entirely different views of the future than the vision of whole-world renewal that Jesus himself proclaimed. In the totality of holy paranoia, their contradictions are resolved in endorsing political domination in the present while envisioning political terror in the future. The anticipation of a future oppressive government is compatible with authoritarian control of the government so long as Christians (of a certain sort) are centered.

Resisting this freedom and the totality that reinforces it begins by defining freedom differently, in the deliverance made possible in Jesus.

RESISTING FASCIST FREEDOM

The path of resistance to theologically charged fascist freedoms is paved by recovering a distinctly Christian sense of freedom. It was Dietrich Bonhoeffer who, after a trip to America, realized that American freedom so often differed from Christian freedom. He wrote after his American trip in the late 1930s of the difference between freedom as possibility and freedom as necessity. For him, the freedom of America was best understood in the liberal and individualist notions of freedom that blur with "freedom to rule" in fascist freedom.

Against this sort of freedom of possibility, he conceived of a freedom of necessity. Back then, in his day of European fascism, Hitler was clamoring about German expansion, or "living space," translated *Lebensraum*. It was the sloganized pretext for the German seizure of Czechoslovakia and the eventual invasion of Poland. A fascist freedom if there ever was one.

Now, we have heard similar calls ourselves today from a resurgent "America First" ethos. This freedom of possibility is everywhere. And dominionist theologies celebrate it as the right of Christians. But against this, we have Bonhoeffer, who suggests not expansive freedom, but the narrow freedom of necessity and obedience as the antidote to pretensions toward power. He writes,

> The freedom of the church is not where it has possibilities, but only where the gospel is truly effective in its own power to create space for itself on earth, even and especially when there are no such possibilities for the church.[24]

Bonhoeffer recognized that the freedom of the church isn't found in a buffet of "possibilities"—i.e., of political programs and seizing power—but in the "necessity" of witness, of speaking of God and his love against the powers that terrorize and tyrannize. But so long as evangelicalism equates winning the culture war *with* witness—it misunderstands freedom. The pursuit of this freedom, says Bonhoeffer, is a denial of the freedom proper to the church.

Conspiracy theories in our time, and in the totality of holy paranoia, trade on false or threatened possibilities to freedom. They invite an anxious response that equates political freedom with Christian freedom. Yet this totalizing convergence of freedoms introduces loss, because it wrongly presumes the freedom of the Christian faith *relies* on the hard securities of political freedom. In our time, many are enlisting authoritarianism as the safeguard for political freedom without realizing this is a house built on sand.

Against all this, authentic Christian freedom raises the necessity of a simple obedience, one rendered to God and rooted in the recognition of the dignity of all as loved by God. This freedom makes possible the pursuit and defense of common freedom in the world. This cruciform freedom isn't of conquest, nor pretensions to power, but rather a form of resistance that can itself testify to God's love for the world that establishes freedom without relying on authoritarian coercion in the process.

THE SETUP FOR A DANGEROUS STORY

Those whose lives and relationships have been altered by the ruining of reality know the pain involved in trying to dispel and displace this totality.

Conspiracism inside evangelicalism is difficult to dispel because it requires incredibly painful dispossessions, not just of fact but faith, too. The uncritical reception of ideologies that, like dimensions of free market capitalism or fiscal conservatism or "color-blind" racism, only tell half the story. Fact alone cannot unseat these primal plot devices of apocalypse, morality, freedom—each is at work, converging into a totality recognized synonymously as "Christian" and "American."

Apocalyptic plot devices, whether the end of the world or a knowing beyond the edge, give conspiracism the hint of divine revelation. Whenever conspiracism is cast in this mold, it relies on the resurrection of Jesus as a prime alternative fact. These apocalyptic devices then ensure plausibility is granted to all forms of alternative or transgressive facts. Apocalyptic plots work by the pitch "They don't want you to know this."

As with apocalypse, so too with individualism. The plot devices of individualism frame how evangelicals understand themselves, and how the world works. Jesus as a "personal" savior is inverted to understand evil as personalized in the world, when the complexity and chaos of evil is far more banal and less recognizable in the distortion of information and propaganda.

There are the plot devices, too, of morality and freedom. Inside this totality, stories of good and evil and freedom find their backing in grounding them in the Christian story. But without critical examination, these plot devices become totalized and rendered untouchable. To be free in an American sense is, in the minds of many, indistinguishable from the freedom of Jesus's deliverance, and therein lies the problem.

These plot devices reveal how totality works as a stand-in for reality, just as they reveal the critical need not for more facts, but a deeper reflection on some of the fundamental assumptions that drive our most powerful, primal stories, which render "reality" to and for many of us.

It's not the Christian story itself, but rather what it has become in the hands of those who profess it, that makes the rise of holy paranoia so dangerous in our cultural moment. And that danger is expressed not just in the holy paranoid perception we've sought to unpack in this chapter. This totality is dangerous because of the anxieties it provokes and the community it creates. This anxious community enters the political arena shaped by falsehood and primed for violence.

Chapter 5

RED-PILLED EVANGELICALISM

> **The Christian who is misinformed; who is subject to the demagoguery of extremists in the press, on the radio or on TV, and who is perhaps to some extent temperamentally inclined to associate himself with fanatical groups in politics, can do an enormous amount of harm to society, to the Church and to himself.**
>
> —Thomas Merton, *Life and Holiness*, 1963

In the 1999 film *The Matrix*, the protagonist Neo is given a choice. The choice is between two pills, one red and one blue. His options are clear, but consequential. If he takes the blue pill, Neo goes back to the way things were. The path of the blue pill will erase his revelation of "the Matrix" and its simulated reality. He'll return to the simulation without remembering this glimpse behind it all. But then there's the red pill.

If Neo takes the red pill, everything changes. He can no longer return to the simulation. He exposes himself to risk. He becomes awake and enlightened to the "true" nature of reality. The red pill commits Neo to a quest, rescuing humanity from enslavement. Everything that follows in this multi-movie series hinges on this choice.

Perhaps it's little wonder that conspiracist culture invokes the language of "red-pilled" to describe its enlightenment. This language seizes on the label "conspiracy theorist" for legitimacy rather than liability. The "red pill" not only signals a conversion, it marks an entry into a community.

The word "church" in the Bible comes from the Greek *ekklesia*, or "called out ones." But in the case of the Christian conspiracy community, it isn't the Word of Jesus that calls this community into being. It's a rogue word with a rival community, converted into a movement that claims the name of Jesus for itself, that organizes under a "biblical worldview," but is—itself—deeply rooted in falsehood and violence.

The way this community takes shape involves a subversion of Christianity itself into a domesticated religion that endorses nationalism, authoritarianism, and strains of late fascism. We've already touched on the idea of this red-pilled evangelicalism, but I want to press deeper into the practices that perfect this totality and its community.

From climate denialism to stolen elections to secret cabals, the entry into the conspiratorial reality mimics what Christians call "conversion," and the slogan of choosing the red pill is a distinct metaphor for and proof of this conversion.[1]

I use the word "mimic" because there is more than just a comparison to be made between the two. The totality of holy paranoia *mimics and in fact demands* conversion. This conversion that not only feels deeply familiar and faithful to many evangelicals, who will remember the altar calls and pivotal prayers for salvation of their origins, this conversion to conspiracy is taken as the *continuation* of a more primal conversion to Jesus Christ.

The Greek word for the call to salvation through repentance is *metanoia*, a key theological term for the conversion event. That this word sounds so familiar to *paranoia* isn't a coincidence. If *paranoia* means literally "split-minded," then *metanoia* describes the "changed mind."

But *metanoia* can also communicate a wider vista. The repentance that marks the beginning of the Christian life is a sort of conversion to all God is, says, and does. It isn't just a change of mind brought about by agreement to certain facts, it involves a *trust* in and *reliance* on God's working.

Totality mimics this sort of conversion. But it reveals itself ultimately to be only cosplay.

I remember once as a pastor being asked by someone considering becoming a Christian, "Do I have to vote Republican now?" This question is a window into the totalizing alliance between Christianity and party and the holy paranoia that conflates the two.

This seeming religious act of choosing the "red pill" mirrors and mimics the conversion many Americans associate with becoming Christian. Stanley Hauerwas calls this confusion and conflation an "identity without difference."[2] That was my world in evangelicalism: what was white was American, and what was American was also Christian. Conversion to Jesus brought all of these things together. This bond is both strengthened and defended by a conspiracism that keeps up with this conversion, producing new knowledge, a new enlightenment—one that always grants access to the room where it happens.

When you fashion party truth as the "red pill" of your conversion, what *appears* to be at stake is Christianity itself. So let me be very clear: conspiracy theory inside evangelicalism *becomes* theological. This transformation has to do with association. Received by Christians, conspiracy theory and its claims about nefarious and shadowy figures are taken as *part* of the same reality depicted and described in the Scripture. This leads us to the next plot device, how conspiracy theories mimic how evangelicals read the Bible as a text to be decoded before it unlocks its secrets.

CODED HOLY TEXTS

When I was a kid, one of the earliest memories I had of church was on Wednesday nights screaming, "THE BIBLE IS THE WORD OF GOD." In my fundamentalist church, this belief was drilled into us as young kids.

I still revere the Bible. But I've also come to believe that Jesus, not the Bible, is God's Word—this is the Scripture's own testimony. And it's the Scripture's witness to Jesus that carries authority—not questions of cosmology or the age of the earth. But not all agree.

Many evangelicals have elevated the authority of Scripture to the status of what critics call "the fourth member of the Trinity," meaning the written words of Scripture occupy a divine place unto themselves. This misplacement of Scripture affects how it is wielded, and weaponized.

A poll of the second Trump administration in 2025 found that nearly 70 percent of white evangelicals found the "ethics" of the Trump administration to be either "excellent" or "good,"[3] and 57 percent of white evangelicals trusted Trump's words more than any other president.[4] Which is telling considering the weight evangelicals claim for the Bible as a source for morality.

With Bible in hand in the evangelical world, I always wanted to "go deeper" in Bible Study. I think that impulse was good, but it can be misdirected toward malformed handling of the Bible. Daily devotions (evangelical speak for daily Bible readings) could involve decoding veiled, hard-to-understand passages and connecting them to political events.

In evangelical hands, the Bible becomes more than what it is. This isn't to detract from its importance to Christian faith. It's to highlight its misuse—the Bible isn't a cipher to contemporary geopolitics; it does not authorize scientific commentary on cosmology.

For me, as for millions of evangelical Christians and evangelical-adjacent Americans, what was "biblical" could not be questioned. The adjective "biblical" works something like a lockbox. It gets filled with all sorts of claims and all sorts of teaching, on money, on racism, on morality, etc., and then wielded as an unquestionable truth. Because evangelicals believe the Bible is God's Word and not Jesus's, they treat questions on what counts as biblical as a threat.

This way of thinking about and engaging the Bible primes people for conspiracism. Because "biblical" knowledge and "conspiratorial" knowledge come to share similar characteristics. Whether the struggle of devotion, the decoding, the hidden messages, all of it converged in the movement of QAnon in the late 2010s.

Conspiratorial knowledge doesn't need to be factually confirmed as much as it already goes with the grain, or follows "similar vibes" or contours of what the totality calls "biblical" knowledge.

Where did this way of reading the Bible originate? And how does it supercharge conspiracism?

Much of it emerged from the end times theology of dispensationalism at the turn of the century. Partly a reaction against modernist criticism of the Bible and partly a novel teaching in its own right, dispensationalism taught millions of Americans (citizens and Christians alike) that the Christian Scriptures contained coded references to major geopolitical events.

Dispensationalism made it so that a "faithful" reading of the Bible would reveal a "clear" timeline of history that culminates in the second coming of Jesus Christ. And of course this was hard to reconstruct. But the struggle itself had a ring of faith to it. Only by deep, devoted study would the Scripture reveal its secrets. And so a special elite class emerged whose teachings provided special access to these insights.

Only the most "faithful" scholars or pastors (like Tim LaHaye or Hal Lindsey) could discern, for example, that the Gog and Magog of Ezekiel 38 were coded references to the nation-state of Russia and its proxies in the late stages of the Cold War. Now, evangelical influencers play the part of outrage merchants and culture warriors, mixing conspiratorial content with Christian values.

Leading up to our time, novels like *Left Behind* and Hal Lindsey's *The Late Great Planet Earth* shaped how evangelicals approached the Bible like no other academic work in the twentieth century. Their popular commitment to dispensationalism primed wide swaths of the American population to recognize in conspiracism the same sort of knowledge they believed was hidden in their Bibles, too.

But it's not just *how* evangelicals came to read the Bible. It is also how evangelicals *think* about the Bible. By deploying new terms like "inerrancy" and "infallibility" to describe the Bible, evangelicals have constructed a dogma of the Bible. They emphasize the authenticity of the written document as a way to establish the authority of the Bible. This comes at the expense of recognizing Jesus as the *living* Word of God.

And because of this confusion, evangelicals came to invent terms to reflect their particular understanding of the Bible as a truth claim, which were crystallized at a conference in Chicago in 1978 to stare down what was coded as "theological liberalism."

Liz Grant, in her masterful article on the history of the Chicago Statement, writes, "The writers of the Chicago Statement hoped to settle themselves, their families, their churches, and their institutions within the ancient, unchanging text written by God himself. What could be more stable?"[5] The desire for certainty often precedes moving into a totality.

The dogma of inerrancy holds the written words of the Bible are without error (inerrant) and without the possibility of being wrong (infallible). But inerrancy is often expanded beyond the breaking point to include not just what a text *means* but also what it implies or applies. Inerrancy is used as cover for political views that can be entirely dismissed as "unbiblical" strictly because a certain interpretation of Scripture is taken to be rooted in the very inerrant character of the text as evangelicals understand it. Free market capitalism is a great example.

Other theological traditions recognize the Scripture's authority in its testimony to Jesus but not, for example, in its use of ancient cosmology like in Genesis. They accommodate the fact that Scripture makes use of these ancient concepts, while recognizing that in no way does this equate to an authorization of the idea of a flat Earth, for example.

But the fixation of inerrancy means it cannot abide such nuance. Why? Because inerrancy understands biblical authority in a totalitarian way. Its quest to render Scripture as "true" according to modern standards of rationality ends up shattering the larger story the Bible as Christian Scripture tells about God's covenant with his people and God's liberation of the world loved and reconciled in Jesus. This story is shattered in attempts to preserve its "factual" accuracy.

Again, like with the resurrection as the "prime alternative fact," this distinctly evangelical dogma of the Bible comes to serve as another "prime alternative fact" where—armed with a verse or two—one can grant trump card authority to whichever suspicious claim one might want to advance.

The evangelical commitment to inerrancy makes it easy for conspiracy theory to anchor its claims in an isolated text, and so draw "biblical" authority from that touchpoint. What I'm describing isn't what pastors or scholars within the evangelical world would probably recognize as what they mean when they say "inerrancy." But I am depicting the lived, pastoral reality of encountering conspiracy theories among Christians, and the way these narratives draw from the taught evangelical handling of the Bible in America.

By claiming the Bible—and not Jesus—is the Word of God, evangelicals back themselves into a corner where they cannot be wrong since their interpretation of Scripture is considered synonymous with the authority of Scripture.

This is why, when conspiratorial knowledge gets baked into the "biblical" main course, it's impossible to separate one from the other.

In the case of evangelicals in America, faith isn't simply believing the Bible is "God's Word"—faith, for it to be Christian, recognizes Jesus as the living Word of God. This difference illuminates the disoriented *way* evangelicals have come to handle the Bible, rooting the authority of the Bible not in its attestation of Jesus but in its authenticity as a historical document, alone.

This pivot has primed not just the faithful inside evangelical spaces, but vast swaths of the American public, to *seize* the story of the Scripture rather than be shaped by it. This seizure of the story shatters it into a thousand shards that in our day are wielded to sanction authoritarian and totalitarian power.

REVIVAL

The expectation and desire for revival permeates evangelical practices in America. In a variety of denominations, from Baptists to Pentecostals, part of what unites evangelicals in America is an anticipation for a mass renewal, a clear return to God, often demonstrated publicly.

Growing up, it was an expectation that took shape every service. Our weekly services ended with the practice of altar calls. The "invitation"—as it is called—is the essential liturgy for evangelicals who understand conversion as a one-time event. It is that part of the service where hands are raised and decisions made.

And this appeal to invitation and revival made its way to the Capitol on January 6. A participant prayed:

> We've been screaming, we've been fighting, but now I want you to pray with me if you will. Pray! Pray! Pray! Pray! Pray! And if you want, take a knee. . . . Let us pray, let us pray Second Chronicles, chapter 7, verse 14 over our nation. Let us pray. Our father says that if we will repent and pray he will hear our prayers, and he will hear us. Please pray, let us pray: Father God, Father God, we come before you Father, and we pray Lord God for peace on our nation. . . . [Crowds behind begin to chant "Fight for Trump!"] . . . We

pray, God, for justice. We pray, Father, for mercy, Lord God. And we pray, Father God, for our nation to come back stronger than it ever has. We rejoice in you. Thank you, we love you. In Jesus name, Amen.[6]

In all the efforts to interpret January 6—insurrection, riot, tour—we might consider it from the perspective of those who were there: it was a disoriented revival.

Religious historians of America pinpoint two major revivals in Revolutionary America. Considered in hindsight, they've taken on the names "Great Awakening" and—not so creatively—"Second Great Awakening." Like the world wars, the first revival and its sequel *are* connected in a variety of ways. The point isn't to trace that here, but to highlight how conspiracy theory mimics the evangelical expectation of a "revival."

Without getting caught in the muck of what is/isn't revival (entire writing and ministry careers have been staked on that question)—in the evangelical experience, revival is a new beginning. In practice, *mass* revival has been a constant across three hundred years of evangelical history. Even now, the expectation and anticipation of revival is a key animating force in the piety and practice of many denominations that identify with or have been categorized in evangelicalism.

As a practicing Christian myself, I want to keep space for revival, for a sudden and unexpected move of God. But here I offer caution, too. This expectation can be corrupted. Revival can be easily emotionally manufactured. And conspiracy theory, with its narratives that promise not only hidden information, but access into an *ongoing* plot, can seize on this expectation, hollowing it out, and directing it toward other ends.

Sometimes, it is too on the nose. For example, one of the key "claims" of the QAnon conspiracy theory universe was the advent of a "Third Great Awakening" in America. This claim wasn't invented by Q as much as it was integrated into the conspiratorial world fashioned by Q.

Q refers to a user name on the message board 4chan who claimed to have a security clearance and made nearly five thousand posts (called "drops") between October 2017 and December 2020.[7] And data continues to show that evangelicals have absorbed several key tenants of Q. Things like "a coming storm" will soon sweep away society's elites and "political violence may be necessary to take back our country." QAnon isn't simply a conspiracy theory, but its own Disreality complete with a canon of Scripture.

Back in the early 2020s, scholars estimated that nearly one in three self-identified white evangelicals agreed with at least one tenet of the QAnon conspiracy metaverse.[8] While Q itself has faded out, it's easy to see how Q's rhetoric has gone mainstream in popular consciousness. And the best example of this mainstreaming is in the populist appropriation of revival.

The "revival" Q envisioned was spiritual in language but populist in practice, coding Democrats as sinners and in league with demons. Here, there isn't much to discriminate the narratives of Q from the populist ideological expectation of "change"—even God-directed change—that one might normally come to share in evangelical spaces.

I suppose another way of putting it, in terms of political science, is that it is too easy to consider how the appeals of populism-on-the-spectrum-to-authoritarianism can take on the same key as the anticipation of revival. Revolution and revival are too closely associated in the minds of evangelicals, and probably a great deal of Americans whose understanding of Christianity has come via the cultural saturation of evangelical concepts. The divergance of responses to the legacy and activism of Charlie Kirk are an index for how "revival" is synonymous with the escalation of the partisan cause.

"Drain the swamp" is a sort of promised revival and so is "make America great again" and "defend democracy." My point in all this is a modest one: conspiracism doesn't have to name a coming third "great awakening" to mimic and manufacture the Christian expectation for a fresh beginning.

I like what Bonhoeffer says: "People cannot make a new beginning with God, they can only pray for one."[9] This simple observation empties the power and promises of political messiahs. It creates distance, mediated by Christ, between Christian community and the conspiratorial narratives that organize political opposition and activate revolution.

Revival before the living God is actually a whole lot less predictable, and far more radical, than the simple, caricatured narratives of conspiratorial claims. And we need not claim that a new beginning with God doesn't necessitate new ways of thinking about and engaging the political. My point is that the received ways of talking about and anticipating revival are determined by other origins than Christ and his kingdom. But without any way to name and establish the difference this determination makes, millions of evangelicals in churches *or* even non-Christians, through the commodification and cultural saturation of evangelicalism, come to think of revival in ways that stretch the "Christian" to the breaking point.

Expecting revival, evangelicals have collapsed revival of the Church into the expectation of national revival. This collapse tends to prime citizens for a theologically charged fascism. This fascist conspiracism theologically curates the expectation of deliverance, it believes shadowy forces will be overthrown by political messiahs that are inevitably operating in the spirit of antichrist.

What is needed is a way to name and establish the difference of revival before God and the revivals claimed and promised by conspiracy theory in service of totalities constructed by nationalist myths, economic programs, or partisan causes. Because for all their big promises, these lesser hopes are increasingly shaking and shaping our world.

DIGITAL INFOSTRUCTURE

When I was a pastor, I was part of a sermon planning team. And probably about once a year, we planned a sermon series on technology, particularly smartphones and social media. Now, I look back on that and find the silence on gun ownership in churches even stranger. Churches are prepared to admit and address the far-reaching consequences of instruments like phones and social media and platforms on our common life, but when it comes to the instrument of a firearm, suddenly to go there is to get "political."

The contradiction here I hope illustrates the power of conspiracism in reinforcing totality and silencing legitimate questions and deliberation in and among churches. And when it comes to the pervasive influence of phones and digital technology on modern life and our politics, churches have by and large entered only the shallow end of the pool.

So as a pastor, I would offer guidance on principles for phone use. And don't get me wrong, we need wisdom here. But I was not prepared to consider the larger ways our very existence is being transformed and even engineered through our interface with what I call digital infostructure.

The power of totality to create *new* community in digital space primes conspiratorial thinking in a whole novel way. The power of conspiracism, and its mimicry of Christian faith, is that in going down the rabbit hole, you find a pseudo-church, those "called out" into the red-pilled reality, ready and waiting to accept you. These communities can exist within established churches, either as subcultures or as providing the entire church with its prevailing cultural ethos, outright.

But it's not just the internal practices of coded holy texts or expectations of revival that prime people for the community of conspiracism. In the age of a digital revolution, our interface with screens—and particularly how faith claims are framed and encountered *through* the mediating power of socio-digital technology—is just as influential as these practices.

The promise of community is yet another reason facts alone cannot draw someone out of conspiracism. There is a significant social loss in leaving the world of conspiracism behind. In fact, research shows that direct confrontation with conspiratorial claims tends to do the exact opposite—it doesn't convince but only fuels deeper entrenchment with whatever beliefs are being held. The strain this puts on relationships is immense. It's little wonder that, without knowing the dangers of this approach, we are left with ruins, not just of reality, but of relationships and communities.

Conspiracism once again cosplays how Christian faith is experienced: through participation in a community. The New Testament word for this community, and the participation in it, is *koinonia*. This word contains a radical idea tied to a more fundamental concept. That concept is the idea of "the household" found in the Greek word *oikonomia*—where our word for "economy" comes from. *Koinonia* envisions more than just shared possessions in the household; it envisions *joint participation*, a family marked out not by hierarchy (as in the Roman household) but a new house of shared dignity, equality, and mutual responsibility.

When we understand how sociality operates at the end of the conspiratorial mimicry—from conversion to pious decoding to anticipating revival—we recognize that no one really ever does this alone, at least not anymore.

In our present time, the sociality of conspiracism has gone mainstream. If I were writing this book a decade ago, I'd talk about message boards and siloed algorithms. Now all of these are factors, but our digital infostructure has exacerbated their effects with immense scale and speed.

Our vast world of screens and the "internet of things" *create* our sense of community not only by the seemingly inevitable necessity of interfacing with them, but also by *capturing* human attention, *directing* our interactions, and *enclosing* our experience. All of this is *by design*.

In her book *The Age of Surveillance Capitalism*, psychologist and scholar Shoshana Zuboff describes not just the material creation of this digital infostructure, but depicts the logic that drives its expansion. Written in 2014, Zuboff set out to narrate the rise and expansion of companies like Google and Meta from a search engine and social network to something *other*. These companies rely on a logic of expansive capture committed to *data*. All sorts. All types.

Data is the new oil, to put it simply. But it's not merely the accumulation of data that matters, but rather the power inherent to this data and how it enables corporations and individuals to go rogue, bypassing the traditional geopolitical power structures set into place after World War II. Elon Musk is a rogue baron in this sense. From SpaceX to Tesla to X to Starlink satellites, Musk exercises a sort of power that has traditionally been wielded by nations. Through his purchase of X (formerly Twitter), the very idea of "misinformation" has been drowned out by the sloganeering of "free speech." Alongside Musk and Meta's Mark Zuckerberg are less well-known billionaires like Peter Thiel, who runs an intelligence firm called Palantir, which sells data to the defense industry. We are in uncharted territory, a moment of deep change that cries out for deep belonging.

Conspiracism appeals in this moment of change precisely because it offers certainty bound up in community. But what if this polarization is the point? What if a fragmented, divided world reflected in conspiracism is a feature of digital infostructure?

Professor and historian Quinn Slobodian builds on the idea of surveillance capitalism to show how it is reorganizing our political and social world. In what he calls "crack-up" capitalism, Slobodian argues the world is moving toward "capitalism without democracy."[10] It is a world not of states, but "zones" where different sets of rules apply, where certain corporations bring order, not the rule of law.

There are consequences to this zoning of human society. Slobodian writes, "We are being encouraged to live in zones by those who profit most by our abdication from the shared set of responsibilities. A hundred years ago, the robber barons built libraries. Today, they build spaceships."[11] The sort of conspiracism that protects our totalities also primes us to see those *within* our totalities as good, and all outside as evil.

As I watched the second Trump inauguration, which featured Amazon's Jeff Bezos, Meta's Mark Zuckerberg, Google's Sundar Pichai, and of course Elon Musk, it felt as if I was witnessing the inauguration of this surveilling, cracked-up capitalism. The capacity of Google and Meta and Amazon and Starlink or X or Tesla to outflank and outmaneuver democratic oversight (even while championing things like "personal liberties" or "free speech") illustrates their power.

But at a more direct, existential level, the emergence of these corporations or individuals as rogue networks (which defy common accounts of oligarchy or autocracy) threatens anyone who interfaces with their many products and services. Why? These totalities create our sociality and thus *conform* us to extraction operations and the erosions of political equality. Yet, Zuboff warned, it isn't just about extraction of data or the ability to predict it, but also about the ability to modify and dictate behavior to "lock in" a specific sociality and state of affairs, as Slobodian warns.

Where does conspiracism and the totality it serves fit in all this? In a more generalized way, the communities or zones constructed by the practice of surveillance capitalism are socialities of distortion and segregation. Our notion of "people like us" in a time of Disreality is engineered as much as it is experienced organically. Totality reinforces this engineering, rather than challenges it.

What appears as "clear" or "obvious" or "given" often obscures the totalizing capture exercised by systems of domination. These systems sort humanity—our personal and collective life—into a moment where rights are eradicated, people are erased, and human community is destroyed.

My point here is to suggest that the socialities that emerge from totalities are not some pathological community at the bottom of the rabbit hole. Rather, my point is that when we adjust for the broadest possible conception of mimicry—not just conspiracy theory, but also distortion and misinformation and the power of surveilling crack-up capitalism—we find that at many levels we are *all* subject to a religion of our own making, one that mimics and manufactures faith.

Life in the ruins of what we once called reality has unsettled us from much of what we used to take for granted. And for many, finding *belonging* in the midst of these ruins isn't merely an irrational act, but an attempt to survive. I feel like it's important to state that many who find themselves locked into conspiratorial thinking enjoy a deep sense of belonging. And I've sought to show in this final section how, in many ways, much of the concepts of community and sociality emerging in our world require elements of distortion and separation in order to make way for the erosion of political rights in the name of economic expansion.

Ironically, in trying to offer a compelling explanation for a complex world, conspiracy theory ends up being a caricature of the true scale of the chaos. As a caricature, conspiracy theory tends to accelerate rather than arrest these changes.

The certainty it offers is an illusion. So long as conspiracism mimics a "Christian" way of living, evangelicals will manufacture a Christianity conformed to their totality.

Though we stand in the ruins of reality, I want to preview hope. It's a hope grounded in the recognition that totalities may be destroyed, but all isn't lost. It's a hope that grows as we come to *receive* a reality not of our own making.

Chapter 6

CLAIMED BY REALITY

> **You cannot get the truth by capturing it,
> only by its capturing you.**
>
> —Søren Kierkegaard,
> *The Journals of Søren Kierkegaard*, 1854

"They haven't left us much to believe in, have they? . . . I can't believe in anything bigger than a home, or anything vaguer than a human being."[1]

Faced with Disreality, I keep coming back to these words of Beatrice, a fictional character in Graham Greene's classic Cold War novel *Our Man in Havana*. She names the visceral feeling left by Disreality, and its choice between resignation and responsibility.

Maybe this names the stakes for you, too. I hope it does.

On the one hand, we want to throw our hands up in resignation. The pain, the power, the panic brought on by this torrential flood of Disreality, who can push back against it? Facts seem to fail in the face of primal stories.

But then, deeper than resignation, resistance rises, refusing to abdicate responsibility to the truth—always more than fact, but never less. Still, the truth is costly.

James Baldwin lived this. In 1962 he penned an essay naming the responsibility of American artists to "tell as much of the truth as one can bear . . . and then a little more."[2] This responsibility had faltered in his time, and it has stumbled in ours, too.

But now, like then, a future is still possible. How? "Not everything that is faced can be changed," Baldwin wrote, "but nothing can be changed until it is faced."[3] This is what we have been attempting to do: face and name the problem to ask a better question of hope, and the possibility of change.

The totality of holy paranoia in evangelical Christianity has to be named and faced if change is going to happen. I've attempted to do this the only way such naming can occur: from the inside. Because this naming of totality provokes a crisis of faith, of just who Jesus is. This paranoiac Christ—a messiah of American might—is at the heart of the vortex of fake news, alternative facts, and suspicious claims. It's one thing to name it, another to ask: What next?

TO NAME A THING

I'm convinced that the way forward out of Disreality is paved by practices that draw attention to truth in all its forms. Fact-checking, to be sure. But also *and*, better stories, a renewed attention to the power and weight of words.

The tongue, says James in the Scripture, has the power of life and death. Like the rudder on a ship, words direct and determine the course of a life. And James's conclusion illumines the paranoia that afflicts evangelical Christianity in America: "A well," he says, "cannot give good water and bad water."[4]

The worlds of our words can heal, or harm. This primordial power, the power of language, of the spoken word, is being revisited in our time for its capacity to construct a version of reality itself. Totality is, remember, the product of story. You don't have to practice the Christian faith to see this for yourself.

As Anna Dorn puts it, "To name something is never to describe it. It is to decide what it gets to be."[5] She goes on to cite recent neuroscience showing how the neural "processing of proper names and common nouns involves different brain mechanisms."[6] So it matters, deeply, whether someone says "illegals" or decides to call a human being by their proper name. Set inside a story, this act of naming takes on even greater power.

The power of naming from the perspective of neuroscience points to this truth: words make their own worlds. And it's not just neurology or psychology. Quantum physics is slowly illuminating the unpredictability of the natural world. That perhaps nature—what Agamben calls "bare reality"—isn't as predictable as Darwin demonstrated and *more* relative than Einstein discovered. Suddenly, at these new horizons, creaturely consciousness itself appears more mysterious and significant than ever before. And Christian faith isn't silent here, either.[7]

To name something is a power all to itself. It is primordial, the heart of the problem and solution. In the Hebrew Scriptures, God *speaks* over the chaotic water of nothingness, and Creation answers. Godself speaks, and light emerges. This God speaks, and day contains the light, and night contains the dark. The expanse of sky stretches up and over at this Word, and land pushes back the chaotic waters, setting their limits. The land, at this Word, yields plants, and trees, and sea grasses. This Word is answered by planets, and stars, the sun, and our moon. This Word is answered by a cacophony of consciousness—of creatures great and small. And then his Word is answered by creatures of a kind that bears a striking resemblance to Godself. And what does the human ("a-dam") do? The human *names* Creation as an answer to God.

But this story is honest—brutally so—about what this power of naming has become in our hands. Genesis tells the bitter truth that—after seizing the knowledge of good and evil for themselves—the human (a-dam) renames his wife from wo-man (ish-ah, or "of man") to "e-ve"—or "mother of living." After breaking faith with God, the first act of human naming is to reduce and instrumentalize. The a-dam now looks at his partner and names her according to mere biological function, of "making babies."[8] Patriarchy begins with a word, with the power of speech.

The human consequences of our words, and the worlds we form, are laid bare in our history. But there is also the story of God, and the Word of Jesus, that does not leave us to ourselves. There are the totalities we construct, and then there is the reality of God, a fullness we receive. And *this* posture of receiving, rather than domination, makes all the difference.

THE WORD THAT CLAIMS US

The Gospel of John opens with a riff on the ancient story of Genesis. Instead of "In the beginning, God created . . ." readers of John's gospel hear, "In the beginning was the Word . . ." This Word, John says, "is the light of humanity" and the fullness that issues in "grace upon grace."[9] This matters, for everything and all of it.

Disreality leaves many of us exasperated, even incapable of seeing how we could ever claw our way back to the semblance of reality before the ruin. But that is my point:

there is no going back. The death of truth in our time needs a resurrection. Though all the facts in the world seem to be at our fingertips, though it feels as though common reality escapes us, the Christian faith is a provocation of a single point: truth overcomes even death.

This shouldn't legitimize apathy, as it so often has among the affluent. Truth makes life itself possible. Because of this, reality is no longer ours to construct; reality—as the Word of God—is something we receive.

I suppose some will say, "What does all this God talk have to do with the blatant lies and deceptions of Christians who peddle half-baked medical theories or political propaganda?" And I agree with the spirit of the question. Remember, the suspicion and disinformation that rages within holy paranoia is rooted in God talk, in a portrait of who God is and what God does.

But the question is an essential one. What good is theology—what good is God talk—if it doesn't walk and speak to what we have in common? My answer to this well-meaning question is if reckless faith has contributed to our state of ruin and Disreality, I propose that responsible faith can be part of the way forward to a better story, a common good, and a shared reality.

I believe responsible faith offers the ground from which to question and confront conspiracism. And that ground emerges from examining *ourselves*. *Our* suspicion, *our* totalities, *our* proclivities to pathologize.

The change begins with us in our daily, persistent refusal to recognize "truth" as something established by violent, coercive power—be it propaganda or force. This doesn't begin with pointing out where others are wrong. It begins with resisting our own totalizing. And as it turns out, this resistance begins with a refusal to coerce, to opt for violence as a means to establish truth as an end.

If we cannot change anyone but ourselves, if we can only convince through patience and a willingness to dialogue, then the work does not begin with another person and their failure to face truth and fact. It begins with a willingness to be dispossessed of our own certainties, to be provoked into recognizing our own totalities.

I am convinced that Christian faith enacts this sort of dispossession. But no totality dies easily, it is always trying to establish itself by force. And Christianities have done this across the last two thousand years. Whether in the totality of crusading ideology or in today's holy paranoia, lies and violence go together. The truth-telling we are called to in a time of Disreality will expose falsehood and provoke violence. But for Truth to be truth, it does not need to answer in kind.

THE WEIGHT OF TRUTH

This was the insight from one of the great prophets of the twentieth century. His name was Aleksandr Solzhenitsyn.

He was arrested for his political opposition to Soviet communism and sent to the icy Siberian gulags. But he survived.

Solzhenitsyn bore witness to his experience for the world in a Nobel prize–winning book, *The Gulag Archipelago*. In his Nobel acceptance speech, Solzhenitsyn named a hard-won insight into how totalities establish themselves when threatened. "Violence cannot conceal itself behind anything except lies," he said, "and lies have nothing to maintain them save violence."[10] We are witnesses of this bitter truth. We are also paying the cost for our failure to remember it.

From endless claims of "fake news!" that now prime the American population for authoritarian governance to who knows what new conspiracies have taken root since this book was written—all testify to a single truth: the establishment of totalities as "reality" demands violence in defense of their truth. Always.

This is why rhetoric about "foreign invaders" presented as the "true story" of immigration in America demands the constructing of concentration camps. This story, charged by a malformed conspiratorial gospel, claims the name of Jesus to justify the warrantless detainment of political opposition or erasure of people. Lies and violence are bound up together. And the name of Jesus is implicated in it all.

A resistance that tells the truth responsibly understands that truth that needs violence to legitimate itself is simply not true. Christians see this firmly in the Cross, where God's Word, Jesus, reveals God's reconciliation right at the point when humanity turns its back on God. Our words and the worlds they built always opt for this truth established by violence. And in a time of Disreality, this truth of power is everywhere ascendant.

TOTALITIES OF VIOLENCE

The violence that lurks in the depth of Disreality can be found in between two questions on the lips of the Roman governor Pontius Pilate. As he interrogated Jesus, the gospel of John records that Pilate asked Jesus the truth about who he was and what he had come to do.

"So you are a King?" Pilate wanted to know.[11] "You say that I am," Jesus responded, "but I was born to bear witness to the truth. Everyone who listens to the truth hears my voice." You can almost hear the frustration, the exasperation, the pain of Disreality in Pilate's response: "What is truth?"

But a second question brackets the first. After Pilate has Jesus whipped and flogged, he's returned to Pilate for another round of interrogation. The crowd was calling for his crucifixion, but Pilate up to this point had insisted there was no charge worthy of death.

This was until the religious leaders upped the charges. They argued Jesus had called himself the "son of God." This was a title that caught Pilate's attention, for it was a title reserved for Caesar. A backwater revolt in Judea suddenly took on a new dimension: the possibility of a challenger to Rome.

Pilate brought Jesus in for a private audience, wanting to know where he was from. Jesus was silent. Unable to get clarity from Jesus on this charge, Pilate laid bare the stakes. "Do you not know," he asked, "that I have the power to release you, or crucify you?"

Disreality, in all its brutality, advances in the gap right between these two questions: "What is truth?" and "Do you not know the power I hold?" Between these questions is the idea that whatever is *true* or *real* isn't just revealed but also created through the wielding of power.

The Roman Cross was meant to signify the Roman claim to establish reality, to render truth through power. Truth through violence is what Nietzsche named in the nineteenth century when he spoke of the "will to power." Nietzsche famously called this will to power "reality" itself and "the fundamental fact of all history."[12] He captures what many of us assume in talk about the real world—truth established and defended by the exercise of violence.

AN UNOCCUPIED ZONE

Receiving reality from God stands in stark contrast to the will to power. But so long as evangelical Christianity—with its holy paranoid totality and its myths of American might—

persists in its present state, this will to power is taken as something "biblical" or Christian.

In a 2023 interview with NPR, Dr. Russell Moore, the editor of *Christianity Today*, revealed the pervasive, haunted nature of Nietzsche's ghost. He said,

> Multiple pastors tell me essentially the same story about quoting the Sermon on the Mount parenthetically in their preaching—turn the other cheek—to have someone come up after and to say, where did you get those liberal talking points? And what was alarming to me is that in most of these scenarios, when the pastor would say, I'm literally quoting Jesus Christ, the response would not be, I apologize. The response would be, yes, but that doesn't work anymore. That's weak.[13]

I can relate to this experience. A committed Christian once told me, "Look, America is good, but it has to do bad things." Too many are convinced that America's greatness and goodness are dependent on a more fundamental commitment to (to put it crudely) "badassery," and moreover, this violence is portrayed as noble or desirous.

An entire influencer culture committed to this militancy and its vision of masculinity exists to deliver this ethos as something both consumable in and *compatible* with evangelical Christianity.

Elite military units like Navy Seals or Army Rangers or Green Berets occupy an almost mythological place in the American consciousness. This is especially true of evangelicalism where, in 2023, a men's Christian conference featuring Senator Josh Hawley also included a militarized spectacle of a tank crushing cars like a monster truck.[14]

In evangelical churches, the idea of biblical masculinity is often directly associated with the ethos of the military and particularly those of special forces units. I saw this firsthand as a pastor in the slew of men's conferences I often attended or even helped plan, where the keynote speaker (or sometimes the entire conference) was branded through affiliation or association with a former special forces operative.[15]

The special-forces-to-Christian-speaker pipeline is a powerful platform in perpetuating the will to power in and among Christians. And the messaging that makes its way into evangelical churches only strengthens the perception that the end of a "biblical worldview" ultimately relies on the capacity for violent action.

For example, I came across one special-forces-turned-Christian-speaker whose pinned reel on Instagram has over one million views. The following text is cut and overlaid on clips of armed special forces operatives engaging in training exercises on land, air, and sea, not unlike the propaganda reels for ICE and DHS during the second Trump administration:

> [Some are] saying men should be dangerous. By dangerous, [they mean] I should be ready to threaten somebody, to hurt somebody. No. You should be capable of it. But that doesn't mean you should use it. There's nothing to you otherwise. . . . If you're not a formidable force, there's no morality in your self control. If you're incapable of violence, not being violent isn't a virtue.[16]

And to bring this down to earth, this will to power, the idea that what is true is rendered and maintained by violence is an assumption shared not just by evangelical churches who participate in the lucrative speaker circuit. The idea surfaces among the very billionaire elites leading the world into capitalism without democracy. Elon Musk posted the following text to hundreds of millions of people on March 16, 2025:

> You can't truly call yourself "peaceful" unless you're capable of great violence. If you're not capable of violence, you're not peaceful. You're harmless. Important distinction.[17]

We may or may not consider ourselves violent people or commit violent acts. But that is besides the point. I'm not talking about our individual capacity for violence as much as I am speaking of our collective reliance on violence to establish and sustain a particular sort of order and security.

Just think of the phrase "when push comes to shove." Or when things "get real." Even these everyday slogans betray this not-so-hidden assumption that violence and coercion is how what we count on as "real" is created and sustained.

And so when we talk about the "real world," we are living at the intersection of truth, violence, and power. At this intersection, we find a conception of truth that relies less on any objective reality and more on the exercise of violence and power to establish a totality that merely stands in for reality.

This is why I find the theological reflections of Stan Goff so provocative. He offers a compelling theological alternative to the will to power. Goff is a former special forces operative, now Christian theologian. His book *Borderlines* fundamentally altered how I view violence, sex, and gender. He writes, "War is implicated in masculinity. Masculinity is implicated in war. Masculinity is implicated in the contempt for and domination of women. Together, these are implicated in the greatest sins of the church."[18] For Goff, nonviolence isn't some pacifist escape route, but a risking responsibility grounded in Christian faith itself.

Such nonviolence is the creative response of Christian faith and its witness to truth in a world marred by the will to power, including a Christianity malformed by holy paranoia. And how could we conclude otherwise? From CIA black sites torturing Iraqis during the War on Terror, to the Trump White House curating what was titled as ASMR videos of migrants being flown to Guantanamo Bay,[19] to the funding of desolation in Gaza, to elected politicians taking photo ops in front of concentration camps in El Salvador, in all these spectacles there is a lingering and powerful assumption that this spectacle of power and violence establishes what is both real and true.

These words gone rogue create a world without question. But Goff helps us preview how it is this claim at the heart of totality—of truth through violence—that Christianity challenges and subverts.

DATASETS TO CONQUER AND THE STORY THAT SUBVERTS

The facts of human history testify to our bent toward brutality. I am convinced we do not repair totality and its brutality, we are rather delivered from its illusions by a liberating dispossession. And this dispossession doesn't come about by a dataset, but by a story.

Jewish philosopher and theologian Michael Wyschogrod sums it up well: "The promises of God are more persuasive than the facts of history."[20] Data has its place. I'm particularly interested, for example, in the fascinating "Pentagon Pizza Index" that correlates American military operations with surges in pizza orders near the Pentagon.[21]

Data can help us decide, it can give us perspective, it can help us predict or calculate risk. But conquering datasets doesn't promise or provide a glimpse of reality in its entirety.

In a world overflowing with data, we need deliverance, too. John Steinbeck, the great American novelist, knew this when he described industrial farming in the Great Depression:

> For nitrates are not the land, nor phosphates; and the length of fiber in the cotton is not the land. Carbon is not a man, nor salt nor water nor calcium. He is all these, but he is much more, much more; and the land is so much more than its analysis.[22]

One concrete human being, you or me, in all our lived contradictions and complexities, is irreducibly more than all the data compiled on us. The stories that bind us or liberate us are the words that build worlds.

This is why it is significant that we come to receive God's reality as a story. Talk about God's reality that is abstract—as some prime principle or bit of dogma—might lead some to practice a "head in the sand" piety. This piety is little more than a religious cultivation sealed off from the common world, allowing some to persist in our totalities and their reliance on violence.

But to receive God's reality is to reflect on deliverance, and actively rehearse a story with continuity, with stakes in the ongoing venture of how we ought to live. How does this story continue, except in the recognition that Jesus isn't dead, that his rule and reign—marked by mercy and justice—continues to have its witnesses in the world, right alongside those who would shatter this story into shards from which they construct and sanction their own totalities? This is the witness of Christian faith, not to *content* but to a life that flows from this confession.

God's reality bound up in the body of Jesus subverts our totalities. God meets us in the particularity of our lives, not just in burning bushes like with Moses, but in people who cross our path. While holy paranoia speaks of a totalizing myth of everything, God arrives in a body.

The story of God initiates humanity in a startling deliverance: reality isn't something we construct by words or establish by might, but someone we encounter. Nothing could be so counter to the way holy paranoia claims to see the whole. I love how the theologian K. H. Miskotte puts it: "God has a name. . . . God is not the All, but is known as a reality that distinguishes itself *in* the world. . . . God does not appear to us as the most general, that which can be found everywhere, but rather as the most unique, that which can be sought and found somewhere specific."[23]

The Christian story doesn't offer the certainty many claim it does. What it does offer is communion. It doesn't offer omniscience, authority, the right to rule or seize power because of the belief that someone with a Judeo-Christian perspective can "do it better." When the Christian story is enlisted to these ends, the witness of the church ends up being about power and the right to rule, as based in "being right."

Instead, the reality of God is carried on by this story and reveals itself in Jesus as the risen Crucified One who delivers humanity, joining us to a new creation. And this Revelation, according to theologian Cody Bivins-Starr, comes to us "like a cut from within," a specific interruption of our own concrete life, severing us from the stories that had once previously served as the content for our sense of what is "natural" and "real."[24]

Jesus does not give us, as modern people, what we want: airtight, factual certainty. He did not write a book; he fed people and baptized them and sent them as witnesses to a life that is bound up in an ongoing story. This story concerns non-Christians as much as it does Christians, because certainly the story of the conspiratorial gospel affects everyone. But unlike the conspiratorial gospel, the Christian story concerns itself with the flourishing of the common world. The thing is, the flourishing of this common world can feel like the end of the world. But what if that is good news?

The Christian faith witnesses to God's story of reconciliation with humanity as the *true* story of a world we already have in common. I like how theologian Brian Brock puts it: "The only thing the church knows that the world doesn't is who sustains it."[25] This fundamentally alters how evangelicalism thinks about knowledge.

KNOWLEDGE: CONTENT OR COMMUNION?

The reality of God disrupts our totalities not by giving us access into all knowledge but by delivering us for dependence on God. Knowledge isn't concerned exclusively with the mastery of content—and conspiracy produces more content than ever. Christian faith isn't some repository of secret content that outsiders know nothing about. The knowledge that emerges from Christian faith is definitively public knowledge, compatible with the common experience of the world. Jesus is human, after all. Christian knowledge emerges from encounter and communion with God. And this communion makes a claim on us, one that initiates us in a process of discovery, of unlearning. We do not have to fear this.

The Christian faith forms people who recognize reality not as something we construct, but as Someone who claims us. This means, when it comes to the nature of reality, the Christian life doesn't begin with scientific content about geology, the age of the Earth, or the evolution of species.

This is not to discredit these claims! The point is that the content and consensus of the scientific community *alone* do not determine the truth in which Christian faith places its hope. Where science articulates the facts of gravitational forces and planets, where it peers into the quantum realm and its mysterious chaos, faith confesses the reality of Jesus as the risen Word upholding and sustaining all we call real. These are not in opposition, unless science also aspires to totality in the same way as evangelical Christianity in America.

God's reality received through communion is what forms human beings to recognize nature's forces—the chaotic and the controlled—as Creation, the site of God's care, of reconciliation, and in hope of redemption. And this care, this God, isn't "far off but near you."[26] The Word that teaches us to recognize bare nature as something *more*, Creation. And yes, it makes the ask of faith.

REALITY OF DEATH OR REALITY OF RENEWAL?

A glimpse at the state of the world, of our death worlds and our collective violence, of the barren void of nature, how could we *not* but conclude that—left to ourselves—meaning is ours to excavate from our own situation and perception? This was philosopher Albert Camus' conclusion: we must seize on our own existence, otherwise fate and the absurdity of it all would collapse and crush us. Stories pave the path we take through the world.

This Christian faith proclaims as truth a specific story of the world liberated from death and destruction and destined for restoration by the crucified life of Jesus. In this proclamation, Christian faith does not naïvely deny the state of evil and death and destruction. To the contrary, this story invites our trust because of its open acknowledgment of the ruins, and the great need for this renewal. Christian faith endures the universal human experience of death. From the grave emerges a truth that does not need violence to establish its peace. And because of this, Christian faith bids us to boldly believe and confess that a God whose Word wrestles life from death determines that the present state of our world, with its violence, isn't fated or final.

Faith confesses Jesus is reality, and reality is Jesus. And what makes this reality different from our totalities is that it is not one that we *construct*. Reality comes to us in Jesus as something we receive. It is no longer up to us to secure by any means, let alone violence. This is liberation, salvation, good news. God's reality is a reality that *claims* us, an encompassing of a common world in love.

But whenever and however conspiracy theory becomes entangled in evangelical Christianity, it has displayed a tragic ability to distort the dimensions of the Christian story. By stories that trade on power and greed (as in slavery) or on anxiety (as in the myth of the nation), each results in a malformed Christianity that empowers death and so squelches and denies truth.

By conforming Christianity to the needs of authoritarian domination, or totalitarian unity, such a faith betrays the risen life of Jesus. In either direction, the reality of Jesus is put in service of other stories, other realities that claim sovereignty for themselves, and tell their own stories.

When this happens, the reality of Jesus is reduced to a resource, to a principle, to a moral system. It becomes shattered, and we wield its fragments without regard for the whole.

Because this reality *claims* us, it isn't something we *control*.

Nor is it something we handle outside of our own creatureliness. By "creatureliness" I am recapturing what Christian faith says about us, as humans, namely that we are God's children, reliant, dependent, but also sustained. As creatures, in our hands, there can be no *pure* handling of the reality of Jesus. We never escape the confines of our creaturely life, we never arrive at perfect knowledge of "pure" or "objective" fact.

We receive and rehearse this story in the midst of our contradictions, our compulsions, and our chaos—or we do not receive it at all. But of course, there will be those variant and malformed Christianities that believe God's reality is something to be seized, not received. Wielding God's reality as a weapon of coercive conformity betrays the life at its center, the God who rules by stooping to wash feet.

And right here is precisely where conspiracy theory entangled in Christianity pushes back with all its strength. It says, in thousands of voices and refractions, that we must *not* change. That "they" cannot win. The lesser stories it tells corrupt the Christian story at its center. Just like it enslaved human beings in the name of God; just like it preserved the military-industrial complex in the Cold War. Even now, as fractures and revolutions persist around us, we must recognize conspiracism's desire for change as a *nostalgic* one, best illustrated by that tired slogan "Make America great again." And evangelical Christianity has made itself an agent of Disreality by sanctioning this greatness that is experienced by millions as terror.

The political project of Christian supremacy is a dead end because it seeks to wield death and the powers of hell that Jesus himself disarmed in his victory over death. In our hands, the reality of Jesus is inevitably corrupted and corroded and calcified into yet another totality by our attempts to wield it in coercive, violent, and dominating ways.

Instead, we can only participate in and yield to the reality of God, its freedom and its power, the proof of which is the renewal of our minds (Romans 12:1-2), our *way of seeing the world*. In other words, because this reality—this God—*claims* us, we need not fear change, we must expect it.

DANGEROUS DELIVERANCE

Jewish philosopher Abraham Joshua Heschel taught, "Faith is not the clinging to a shrine but the endless, tameless pilgrimage of hearts."[27] This sort of pilgrimage is dangerous, but it also is deliverance. The path of faith is a perilous journey in freedom sustained not by nations, by courts, by zones of free market capitalism, but by the Word of truth—a living word, a reality we receive.

Without faith, the idea of "receiving God's reality" appears rather arbitrary (and at worst hopelessly idealistic). But the faith that recognizes and so receives God's reality is fitted for our time of Disreality. It comes with a different set of questions, it makes dialogue possible, its vision of a common humanity makes for a common world. This isn't faith as some unmoored affinity for spurious spirituality. This is *the* Christian faith.

The faith I'm speaking of is the faith revealed in and by the life of Jesus. It isn't "faith" as some sort of middle ground between fact and fantasy. This faith is defined in and by the Christian story. At the center of this story is a God who suffers violence on a Roman Cross and whose resurrection disarms the power of hell and death's claim on human life.

I suppose this is the opportunity to answer what I'm sure is the slow-burning question that you probably have: Why do I still understand truth by the Christian story? Why—after all we've surveyed so far, all the raging totality, all the damage and distortion—do I still find credibility in the incredulous story of Jesus?

The short answer is simple: I've been converted, delivered, countless times. And this conversion issues in a conclusion that a common world isn't just possible, but promised. Speaking now as a "former" pastor who serves in a little but meaningful Christian community in Tampa Bay: I've become a Christian all over again. A life of ceaseless conversions, a movement, a pilgrimage to God.

I admit, it is pilgrimage of pain, of unsettling peril. For me, it involved the realization that defending the "evangelical" label and movement against those who bear the mark of its destructive impulses—who live under threat of its undoing—was a denial of my baptism itself. I didn't have the language for this—and I'm still learning—but I gained permission through a provocation of a friend who suggested that even apostasy from one thing can be conversion to God.

I've come to the end of my faith countless times, only to find the God of Jesus Christ—again, but different. I don't think God changes, but I do. Like Elijah, that beat-up and exhausted prophet who went to Mount Sinai expecting to see the same God who met with Moses in fire and thunderings and smoke centuries before, but was met by a God whose Word was a piercing stillness. I, too, have found this God to be faithful and free—undomesticated love and mercy.

The more I glimpse of the horizons made visible by the *story* of this God—its ebbs and flows, its surprising interruptions and unsettling, startling interventions, its power—the more I remain convinced of—hopeful and trusting in—God's acts of deliverance as *facts* worthy of worship, not just rational assent. That's the difference of Christian faith, not a denial of facts but giving your life to being determined by the *fact* of God's mercy in Jesus.

This mercy, this justice, this God reconciles us to a better story, one that dares believe reconciliation and redemption as the true story of the world. Not a world of us and them, but a world sustained by the Word of God in love. And so I can dare to suggest that *this* story brings a common hope and builds a common world that is *good* news to those who have been on the receiving end of so much pain, panic, and unjust power from those who—like me—have taken this Name in vain, to use for our own purposes, to wield as words gone rogue, raging with incredible cost and consequence.

It's God who has called me out, and called me back to this truth, and the story that reveals it. A story that speaks of liberation from Pharoah's Empire, as much as authoritarians today. A story that rises and falls in the outcome of a brutal crucifixion outside a Roman-occupied city. Not a sealed tomb, but an empty one—a reality revealed, a story told, one that is ongoing and captivating.

To be shaped by this story today, to receive it and rehearse it—not as content, but in communion—is to be open to the stories of immigrants, to express solidarity with the oppressed, to join with those fighting for justice. All these dimensions and more arise not from some comprehensive view of all reality, but from the human being of Jesus who is God with us. Beatrice was right. This is a reality we can believe in.

The truth of it all compels me like no other. It's a Story that still speaks with a word that offers a way forward out of Disreality and holy paranoia.

I think David Bentley Hart puts it well. He sees the reality of Jesus issuing "an urgent call to all persons to come out from the shelters of social, cultic, and political association into a condition of perilous and unprotected exposure, dwelling nowhere but in the singularity of this event—for the days are short."[28] This perilous position isn't a place from which we discard facts, but discover them anew.

Deliverance, salvation itself, in the Christian faith involves an endless conversion into the "reality" of Jesus Christ and its meaning for the world—not for the enclave of insiders who possess the secret truth. Christianity, in the words of Brian Brock, "provokes different ways of paying attention to the social and material world that already exists."[29]

Evangelicals have emphasized conversion, but reduced its radical, re-cognizing demands, claiming instead to "know" or possess the truth as "biblical" content. Seizing the truth for yourself always severs communion with God. Why? Because it claims a prideful certainty, believing that when what you are is "biblical," then you can never be wrong. This totalitarian certainty of evangelicalism dispenses with the need for faith, because it already *knows*.

On the other hand, when we realize that conversion is a constant upending of our certainties, a severing of all that once claimed the "right" to determine us, then the Christian faith is just an ongoing process of learning to recognize this dispossession as salvation. But violence lies so close to us. The temptation to reduce the Christian story by rendering it as a totality and to defend it through force is always present, and potent.

We resist this temptation by enduring the dispossession of our certainties and practicing the prayerful anticipation of God's reality, recognizing the liberation that reality isn't ours to construct, but receive.

Here, we become the sort of people hospitable toward each other, because we recognize all people have a future in God. This reality changes everything. It frees us from corrupted suspicions toward what I call good suspicion, a perspective and practice fit for a time of Disreality.

Chapter 7

TOWARD A COMMON WORLD

> **A poem cannot stop a bullet.**
> **A novel can't defuse a bomb. . . . But we**
> **are not helpless. . . . We can sing the**
> **truth and name the liars.**
>
> —Salman Rushdie

I kept a letter sent to me by a congregant at my last church. It was during the pandemic, and we had hosted a virtual prayer night. Each pastor was assigned a particular topic. Mine was the Virginia governor, who, at the time, was a registered Democrat.

I led a prayer for the governor, asking for God's guidance and blessing. And that was it. The whole thing was over in a matter of minutes, a quick video call. Until a few days later, when the letter came. Criticism that last year was quick and constant, so I anticipated another round as I opened up the flowery card.

But that's not what I found. The letter was a "thank you." The older woman recounted how, when we began praying for the governor, she became angry. But then anger gave way to conviction, as the woman realized through prayer that here was a human being she did not want to pray for. She thanked me and told me God changed her mind.

The church can make this common world possible. But it can also grind this possibility to a halt. Once we name and face the difference between the conspiratorial gospel that tries to construct reality and the reality of Jesus that we receive, then the telling and practice of this *better* story can displace the anger, the zeal, and the certainty that converges in conspiratorial Christianity.

The stories of conspiracism are fundamentally divisive, while the story of Christian faith is fundamentally inclusive and expansive. In conspiracy, there's always a "they" out to get "us"—and there are plenty of chapters/verses to sanction this view, if you're looking for them.

As stories, conspiracies thrive on opposition and division. And this sort of binary pervades the evangelical totality, where culture warring is just simply a way of life.

As I was preparing this book, I came across a story close to home that illustrates just how deep this way of thinking goes inside of evangelicalism. I think it resonates with many who carry the pain of reality in ruins wrought by evangelical Christianity.

My sister-in-law recounted how, growing up in California, she attended a Christian summer camp that took culture warring to another level. During the week, campers underwent a simulated kidnapping and persecution scenario. Camp counselors, normally full of smiles and ready to help, would get decked out in all black, with ski masks, and wield cosplay firearms.

Counselors would wake up the campers when it was still dark, yelling and brandishing their weapons. They'd shout at campers, "Do you believe in Jesus?" The goal was simulating the sort of persecution Christians faced in various places around the world.

Then, campers would walk to chapel, and have to pass simulated "checkpoints" where, to get past, they had to concoct a good enough lie to convince the counselor-turned-guard that they weren't going to church. My sister-in-law told me she went through one of these simulated checkpoints with a friend who, for obvious reasons, was scared and nervous. She made a light joke to keep her friend preoccupied, but suddenly was singled out for "not taking it seriously enough" by a camp counselor.

It didn't end there. Once they got to the chapel, my sister-in-law was called out from the stage in front of the entire camp. She was turned into an example for the rest, someone who wasn't "serious" about Jesus, or the threat of persecution.

It is incredibly hard to imagine a common world, a world God loves, when your time in the church is framed by constant antagonism against those outside. Especially when you are indoctrinated to anticipate each and every non-Christian harboring the worst, most violent schemes against Christians.

The totality of holy paranoia forms those within it to practice a corrosive suspicion, one that discards inconvenient facts and deforms attempts at truth-telling. It's a suspicion with many dimensions, drawn from many sources, and you can see the urgency in the story it creates.

Pushing back against Disreality does not call for naivety. For a privileged sense that "everything will work out in the end." No, it calls for good suspicion—the courage to say "I don't know" can be a refusal to go along with the lie and its violence, it can give rise to solidarity with those who live under threat, it can point to a deeper knowledge of truth—always more than the facts, but never less. This simple honesty of good suspicion is the building block for a future beyond the ruins of reality.

This practice of good suspicion is hard. It's easy, we've learned, to pathologize those who persist in conspiratorial thinking. And this pathologizing goes two ways: against them ("they're crazy!") and "for" whoever "us" is.

It casts this "us" as enlightened, as possessing all the

facts. It's hard to imagine a way forward when you feel like you have a grip on reality and "those people" over there do not. But believing God's reality is the Word sustaining the world loosens our grip on the totalities we cling to. God is *liberating* us to consider the facts all over again.

This posture cultivates a *good* suspicion, the courage to say "I don't know" that makes the pursuit of a common world possible. This is far more modest than inviting people to inhabit an objective reality, as if we could even see such a thing in its entirety—we cannot! But a common world, one open to the facts, and more importantly to the *process of* learning and unlearning, isn't far from us.

In this chapter, I want us to consider what it takes to pursue a common world together again. To live in a way that is slow to discard inconvenient facts and quick to recognize we have much more to discover. This sort of common world makes political change *possible*, but it is a common world that first demands we become a different sort of people[1] who are practicing *good* suspicion, who are quick to say "I don't know" on the one hand and busy living for the good of the marginalized on the other.

ON SUSPICION

In being delivered from our own totalities, and particularly the totality of holy paranoia, we have reason to revisit what it means to "be suspicious" in a time that calls for resistance to authoritarian propaganda. The common world we can move toward demands a different sort of suspicion than the kind organizing holy paranoia right now. And by examining the counterfeits of suspicion, we make clear the sort of *good* suspicion that makes for a world-in-common.

The word "suspicion" comes to us from Late Latin passed through Old French into English. The word contains ideas and meanings like "mistrust" or "fear." A version of "suspicion" in Latin (I won't bore you with the grammar)[2] also communicates a posture of looking upward. Suspicion is mistrust brought on by directing our gaze *beyond or outside* ourselves.

When we look to how "suspicion" is translated in other languages, we come to an even richer, fuller picture.[3] For example, in Greek, the word commonly translated "suspicion" is *hyponoia*, or literally "under/beyond-mind." The Dutch *achterdocht* can be read *achter-* (behind) *denken* (think). These meanings provide a more robust account of what suspicion is, and what it involves.

Suspicion is defined by an attempt to get behind what is presented or offered at face value. In other words: critical thinking. And so suspicion recruits mistrust, fear, and uncertainty. As we've discovered, this endless drive to "get behind" something cannot always be satisfied—though conspiracy theory and totality tries.

There are many who wear the "conspiracy theorist" label as a badge of honor grounded in this idea of suspicion as a necessary way of approaching the world. I remember once seeing a shirt that read, "I am a Conspiracy Theorist—Pronouns: I/Told/You/So." This uncritical suspicion of everything has no positive content. It is an epistemological cynicism that is incredibly uncreative and predictable.

One of the most enduring lines of classic Hollywood cinema comes from the film *Casablanca* when Police Inspector Renault shouts, "Round up the usual suspects!"[4] Conspiracy theory performs this same basic function as an act of storytelling.

The stories of America nursed inside the evangelical totality are primed to cast certain lives as dangerous or deviant, and therefore more justly punished or marginalized. We saw some of this in surveying the untold history of conspiracy theory across evangelicalism.

But here, I want to speak specifically on corrosive suspicion, and its recovery in pursuit of a common world. But we cannot do this, we cannot pursue and create a provisional common world fit for political action without understanding the corrupting typologies of suspicion at play in our present.

IDEOLOGICAL SUSPICION

Ideology is a concept that seems to mean everything, and nothing. For conservatives and progressives alike, ideology is the problem. I like how political philosopher Jason Blakely describes this paradox in his book *Lost in Ideology*:

Ideology is a snake swallowing its own tail; it is an idea that consumes itself. Indeed, what many people think of as the obvious definition of ideology is nothing more than one more flower growing inside their ideological garden. Every time we seek to rein in ideology, we end up expanding its scope.[5]

In his book, he depicts ideology as "stories about the significance or meaning of social and political life."[6] And each story, produced by a culture, is a map-making project. Ideology, like the maps produced by the earliest modern colonial ventures, promises a picture of the whole. Ideology is a mapping of reality in narrative form. Ideology as map making is a helpful analogy, authentically capturing ideology's claim of having captured all of reality.

But how do we experience this capture ourselves? We experience ideology as simply what is *obvious* or *clear*. We tend to accuse our enemies of having ideologies, mere stories; but us? We have principles! And yet, ideology is everywhere. It is more a home we inhabit than a set of buffet options we consciously choose. Theologian David Bentley Hart echoes this when he observes,

> We are shaped by what we desire, and what we desire is shaped by the material culture that surrounds us, and by the ideologies and imaginative possibilities that it embodies and sustains.[7]

The material affluence and convenience that marks American life warms us to an ideological read of the world and our place in it. This isn't just ideology as a set of propositions or principles. This ideology functions in the way maps do—of reality in totality. And this is something we *experience* long before we ever *consciously assent* to its claims.

Ideology is why propaganda has such power. The story told *about* America, the one that appears most "obvious" or "right" to the majority of Americans, can provide the content for all sorts of propaganda, for the legitimation of power and the normalization of the unthinkable perpetrated on its behalf, at its behest.

The preeminence of ideology, at the level of our personal and communal experience, means it's not necessarily something we can claim to ever escape. Instead, ideology is something with which we must wrestle in an ever-expanding awareness of its hold on us. Ideology claims to offer omniscience while closing the door on everything outside of its artificially rationalized map of reality.

As we consider "totalities" as stand-ins for reality, we cannot consider them without the key ingredient of ideology, both its content and the adhesiveness it offers to maintain that sense of comprehensive integrity.

So to get practical, ideology is the reason why one person sees a protest and thinks, "That's dangerous," while another reflexively thinks, "That's healthy." It is reflexive, and reactive. But we come to *experience* this reflexivity and reactivity as something else: *certainty*. This certainty is illusory. But that doesn't mean it lacks potency.

For modern people whose lives are oriented by and mediated through digital infostructure, ideology provides the scripts for what, to us, seems obvious and clear, even good and just. To the *facts* that matter and the ones that don't. Ideologies are then something like communal algorithms, the narratives that render an account of reality and prefigure the sort of social morality necessary to stave off social collapse.

Because of this, ideology yields a corrosive form of suspicion. It corrodes our ability to encounter difference by contributing to a totality that claims to see things in their entirety. Within totality, people do not encounter difference; it is only defined and divided. It preemptively destroys that which contradicts our own assumed commitments or assumptions. This destruction can be through willed ignorance, through silence, or projection.

Ideological suspicion relies on projection. Because ideology sees nothing beyond its own horizons, everything it suspects of what it cannot understand is understood through the categories it alone has on offer. It is close-mindedness,[8] not out of a failure to think for itself, but more of a failure to invite new categories to the table.

This is how ideological suspicion lends plausibility to conspiracy theories: as a way to keep totality intact. Ideology is why so many Christians can reflexively read "conservatives" as an ally or "liberals" as the enemy, without a thought for what these terms mean when claimed by a singular human being whom they encounter as a complex person. This reading is unreflective, knee-jerk: a rounding up of "the usual suspects."

Ideology renders complex, concrete human beings as two-dimensional, like cardboard cutouts, inside a totality. If someone questions the veracity of a particular conspiracy theory, especially one projected *against* people who are coded by the prevailing ideology as outsiders, well then the act of questioning itself can be construed as support in favor of the outsider. This is how ideological capture and corrosive suspicion work together.

The danger should be apparent. While none of us can *escape* ideology as the essential component of totality, we can *recognize* ideological capture of our imagination by how we come to name and narrate things around us.

Ideology offers a corrosive form of suspicion that emerges to code anything and everything in terms of its own reinforcement. Blakely's analogy of a snake consuming itself is spot-on.

The ideology of capitalism, for example, codes any conversation about collective responsibility as "communism." We could go on listing -isms all day. The point isn't to check each and every -ism as an ideology. The point is to reflect on how these -isms have all contributed to what we reflexively think is "clear" or "obvious" or "just" or "good." The danger here, too, is that even the text of the Scripture can be reduced to the content for ideological reinforcement. Even those who read the Scriptures *seriously* can do so *unaware* of how ideology codes fragments and bytes of Scripture toward the reinforcement of its own premises.

NATIONAL SUSPICION

Closely related to ideological suspicion is the sort of suspicion cultivated by national citizenship. This suspicion is what enabled evangelist Billy Sunday to preach anti-immigrant messages during World War I.

Pervasive ICE raids are given sanction not just by executive directive but more subtly by the insidious spread of conspiracy theories about immigrant invasions that mobilized a mass of Americans to vote for Donald Trump.

The concept of nationhood and the power of the State expressed through particular structures are both arbitrary. National identity, national borders, national sovereignty—none of the political structures of our time are divinely sanctioned. But the sort of suspicion cultivated by a commitment to these structures specifically, and more generally the nation (the represented people) and the State (the governing power), can itself transgress on Christian ways of organizing life together that rely on truly encountering another human being.

We assume that national citizenship precedes personhood at our own peril. We've already explored how theology helps us recover a common humanity by glimpsing God's welcome through adoption and humanity's inherent dignity belonging rooted in that act. This ground helps us parse where national suspicion comes to stand in as an antichrist position in our present time.

The suspicion that emerges from the nation-state assumes too much about its power to be readily trusted. And this suspicion codes anyone deemed "outside" the arbitrary borders or boundaries of political life as people for whom we are not somehow responsible. To categorize all this as "globalism" projects ideology where, instead, theology is trying to provoke a disillusion and dispossession over our assumptions of the way things are, and so need to stay.

National suspicion has, at nearly every turn, cultivated the most pernicious and dangerous sort of conspiracy theories. And in so many ways, it invites the logic of national security to displace, for Christians, the logic of human solidarity that emerges from Christ's cry on the Cross: "Father, forgive them, for they know not what they do." Are we really to believe God leaves this prayer unanswered?

When the Scriptures speak of proper Christian respect for governing powers, they do so with a truly dizzying array of possible political arrangements in view, recognizing the acts of God taking place in *any* sort of political arrangement.

The point here isn't to descend into political theory but

to insist that the suspicion that emerges from commitments to "the nation" has no grounding basis in the suspicion that should and ought to characterize Christian discipleship. Imagine, if you will, the Church in America as a place that reflects the God who, as Peter proclaimed in Acts, "shows no favoritism."[9] It would be a community of and for the poor, the marginalized, and the exorcised. Why? "Isn't that reverse-favoritism?" No! It is the righting of the scales that remain unjustly weighted in our time.

Awake to the reality of this God, we cannot afford to filter our encounters with others through the provisional and temporary lens of national identity, treating it as the first and last thing.

CODED SUSPICION

Paul wrote to a group of Christians in the city of Corinth. In his letter, he told them, "We don't yet see things clearly. We're squinting in a fog, peering through a mist" (1 Corinthians 13:12).[10] Paul's point was to temper their blazing, blinding, and ultimately malformed confidence back into a posture of humility and faithful love.

There's an eschatological or apocalyptic element to Paul's teaching. The here and now of the Corinthians was characterized more by sensationalism than love, more blazing erudition than fellowship. And the combination of sensationalism and erudition had sowed deep, deep division. All this insight, Paul said, was actually *harming* the unity of this Christian community, which had forgotten love.

There is a suspicion that pulls on most of us today that leaves us more divided, more polarized, and more certain that we are right. If the faults of the Corinthians were their emphasis on special gifts, on the spectacular manifestations of enlightenment, then perhaps ours is our smug zealotry that comes less from our intellectual prowess, and more from the process of algorithmic sorting.

In a world increasingly segmented and organized by algorithms and artificial intelligence, *everyone* "is squinting through a fog"; this is the effect of algorithms on our perception and suspicion. At the level of everyday life, we understand less and less of how algorithms operate, while we have come to rely more and more on their recommendations and suggestions.

What algorithms offer is *culturally* compelling: the experience of efficiency and the illusion of autonomy. Through their endless sorting of content, things we like and hope to buy, algorithms can present technology as the peak of efficiency. They seem to clear away clutter; they surface what is "clear" and "obvious." And so, when they present us with options or choices, we forget that the presentation of these choices has less to do with our autonomy and *more* to do with coded predictability.

And so, over time, we tire of *real* choice and *concrete* responsibility. Deliberation is inefficient. Wisdom takes time. Decision is too risky. Even more, we grow less patient with difference, with others whose algorithms are not like ours, whose experience and existence seems to interrupt the ceaseless flow of choices that present to us as freedom. This experience and perception of the world curates its own sort of suspicion, too. And its edges are more defined—they are sharper, and less blurred.

This illusion of certainty is more the state of our own confinement. This is life according to the algorithm. An algorithmic perception of our life presents as affluence and convenience. And few of us are prepared to break out of this precious illusion. The suspicion generated by this perception is profoundly corrupting. The more we interface with and consider our perception of reality through the sorting of algorithms, the more we are shaped by a suspicion that sees inefficiency, difference, and smallness as things to be overcome. Trapped in our worlds, we never think to cross lines of difference. We are formed to be suspicious of this journey, and to resist it with all our might.

CORRUPTED SUSPICIONS

The totalities that contain the content of ideology, the citizenship of our nations, and involve our interface with technology can all combine to create a potent form of corruptive suspicion. I'm not suggesting this is always the case. It's just that by laying out these other forms of suspicion, I wanted to illustrate how not all mistrust, not all suspicion is, well, to be trusted.

We should be more suspicious of suspicion!

There are so many potent forms of mistrust that present to us as tools to find our footing, as means of survival, but most of them leave us unprepared to encounter each other, simply and honestly. More than this, these suspicions look upon that unsettling provocation that is the Christian witness to reality as something to be avoided at all costs!

The suspicion of the nation presses back against the faith that speaks of the kingdom of God. The suspicion of ideology presses back against the faith that carries with it an appreciation for mystery and exposes its illusions of certainty. The suspicion of algorithms can lead us to reject the way of Christian faith for its supposed inefficiency.

But there is hope. We can yet speak of *good* suspicion that sets us back on our feet, with courage and conviction to name, confront, and resist the stories that emerge to weaponize our fears and provide the illusion of certainty only by posing a threat to our neighbor. Let us look now at *good* suspicion as the path toward a common world.

GOOD SUSPICION

I once sat on the platform for a funeral of a man in New Orleans. I was in my twenties, a white pastor, invited by friends of the deceased, a Black man, to offer a prayer at the service. Before I did, I sat and listened to an elder Black clergyman, probably fifty years my senior, who had ministered in New Orleans long before I was born.

In his message, he spoke of "the white man" of St. Charles Avenue. He condemned white corruption in the city (the deceased had been a long-standing chief in Mardi Gras parades, something of a public official in New Orleans terms). And sitting on that stage, I was made aware, distinctly, of myself as white and this moment as an opportunity for me to listen, observe, and learn.

This clergyman helped me understand that suspicion has helped people survive oppression in America and, in this way, isn't only purposed but deeply meaningful. Black communities in New Orleans would do well to be suspicious of the government, as history would attest. And history is full of stories that, when told in full, would create a perception and suspicion that is characterized by legitimate mistrust and distrust.

Take the US government's Tuskegee Trials starting in 1932, an unethical health study that took place across forty years and was performed without the consent of over two hundred African American men in Alabama. Their cases of syphilis were studied and *left untreated* even after the advent of penicillin.

Take Watergate, and the corruption of the Nixon administration. Take the Iran-Contra affair. Take the appearance of the Biden administration's refusal to honestly portray the president's condition to the American people until a debate seemed to remove all doubts.

The America experienced by the Indigenous community, by Black Americans, by immigrants, demands vigilant suspicion. And this suspicion can erupt, expand, and evolve in ways that might give credibility to conspiracy theory *precisely because* of what has been revealed in the past. A backward glance at history can nurse mistrust and calcify distrust—which isn't easily unseated.

This is why I have been speaking not just on the need for good suspicion on the other side of our totalities, but also on the need to pursue a common world as those delivered from totalizing certainty and its oppressive consequences. After all, how can mistrust be alleviated—without truth?

I want us then to consider good suspicion in three dimensions. These are confidence, courage, and conviction. Like Jesus said when tempted in the wilderness, "Man does not live by bread alone, but by every Word that comes from God" (Matthew 4:4). The bread of our own stories and own perceptions awaits the Word from God.

So what makes good suspicion good is its willingness to doubt ourselves, to recognize our deliverance from totality as liberation; good suspicion welcomes the divine sabotage of our securities, a divine siege of our totalities.

Because reality is God's, we are liberated from the tyranny of totality, from having to explain and synthesize it all—the chaos and the complexity—and the means of violence we use to establish and defend them. Good suspicion is only possible then in lives determined by faith, not fear.

Remember that slogan for the pandemic? "Faith over fear!" It was used to flout any and all public health advice. But good suspicion is freed from the assumption that we have all the answers. It sets us on the path toward a common world where both fact and truth are not hidden, and makes possible the alteration of our assumptions.

So we talk about good suspicion because we have confidence in God's commitment to curating better vistas from which we can perceive his ways of sustaining our lives. This disrupts propaganda. It demolishes what passes as reality. This confidence is the first dimension that defines good suspicion.

Confident that we are receiving reality from God, that we are claimed by it, we gain the courage to say "I don't know." Nothing could be more disruptive to conspiratorial thinking than critical recognition of our limits. But let's be clear—this isn't willed ignorance or pious indifference. Good suspicion is rather the courage to say "I don't know" to coercing and propagandistic narratives.

Confident in the story of God, receiving clearer vistas of reality, suddenly we have the freedom to learn and recognize all the claims that offer quick and easy answers, those that seize on slogans and appear obvious or contrived. This recognition gives rise to a powerful resistance. The common trope "Do your own research," which involves hours spent on YouTube, ends up being not nearly as subversive as recognizing our limited ability to be able to know or claim certainty over what is complex or even hidden.

Good suspicion raises the possibility of trust, the simplicity of honesty, and the path back to mutual commitments to one another that rest in a common understanding of truth and reconciliation. To learn to say "I don't know" in this way isn't head-in-the-sand piety, but the pathway to responsibility. By modeling humility, we take ground for honest, courageous action in solidarity with those whose existence is distorted by falsehood and threatened by violence.

In the confidence that we are receiving reality from God, and the courage to say "I don't know," good suspicion is marked by conviction. The Latin root of conviction carries for us the idea of "overcoming." And so good suspicion is a path of overcoming the logics that entrap us, the stories that enslave us, and the anxieties that threaten to strangle us.

Tragically, John's words in Scripture, "This is the victory that has overcome the world—our faith" (1 John 5:4), noted a long, storied legacy of being made to serve causes of domination and violent, militant triumphalism. This is, admittedly, much of church history. But the Christian faith promises a manifestation of judgment that rights every wrong, and this judgment (we are wont to forget) *begins* with the church.[11]

Christians have wrongly understood this as our prerogative to *issue* judgment. And this certainty, along with the totality it constructs, blinds us to the simple fact that Christian faith actually confesses the opposite. The church is simply the place, the people, in whom the judgment of God is both enacted and expected. In this place arises a truth-telling that is *more* aware of our human fallibility and tendency to water down the veracity of truth, not less.

Good suspicion renews the hope and expectation that "the world" overcome isn't the dangerous "other" who lurks in the shadows. Good suspicion begins with not a them, but you, me, us. It lives in an increasing awareness of the difference between the things we want (or need) to be true, and Truth itself.

A DIFFERENT SET OF QUESTIONS

As I attempt to envision what good suspicion offers toward the common world, for all of us, I want to begin with a simple observation: Each of us lives complex and multilayered lives. We are mysteries to ourselves.

This is what gives me pause every time questions like "What now?" or "How should we live?" come our way. And don't get me wrong. These are good and right questions. What gives me pause is quick answers and fast reactions, the kind reflected in conspiracism and totality.

If we were to reduce good suspicion to a static set of principles, we'd prime ourselves for another new dogma. But life is messy and anything but static. None of it conforms readily or willingly to the schemes or systems we impose on it.

What is real, I've claimed, is God's reality. And this reality actually claims the world as the true story. But this reality stands contrary to a totality that we create and control. Jesus claims us in a way that loosens our grip on the perceptions we construct and rely upon to render reality with a sense of certainty.

We are rarely able to grasp the meaning and measure of our own lives, much less the broader strokes of history. And even though the Christian faith draws our attention to Christ as history's meaning, this faith does not promise an omniscience that eradicates the need for faith.

Good suspicion isn't perpetual uncertainty. And so when it comes to applying good suspicion, the confidence, courage, and conviction that come with believing reality are God's freeing us to say "I don't know"—well, so what? How does this prepare us to be the sort of people who make our way in the ruins of reality?

I don't want to come at dogma with more dogma. I want to come with practices saturated with and by attention to the Christian faith. These practices are, I think, means and ways of orienting ourselves to the contours of our lives in contact with the story of Jesus.

And so when it comes to applying good suspicion, I want to suggest that questions are a better place to start. Questions are more easily carried into all sorts of concrete and complex lives, in all their varied responsibilities and unique relationships.

These questions are like pebbles in the shoe, meant to annoy us, thorns of doubt in the midst of all our certainties. In so many ways, these questions can generate fresh, humble perspectives when we're faced with new (or old) knowledge. They can be, I think, the grounds for fresh practices, for a revival of healthy suspicion flowing from immersion in the Christian story into the practices of a community.

So what follows is a set of questions designed to cultivate good suspicion. They aren't meant to be exhaustive. Instead, I hope they're generative. Add to them. Subtract from them. But at large, I think they will be useful. They'll provide a common ground for conversation between people, yes. But I see their most primary use in asking them of our own selves.

Why do I want this to be true?
Or, why do I need this to be false?

The practice of good suspicion is alert to when incoming information seems to confirm (or threaten) our perception. This is especially true when information comes from varied or less-than-reputable sources. But I have more than information literacy on my mind here. This question doesn't just speak to our sorting of facts and examining sources of information—though all of this is good and helpful!

At a more primal level, this question speaks to our desire. To our way of submitting suspicion to our perception, rather than allowing our perceptions to be challenged, reworked, and renewed. This is part of what the Christian life entails. We've said as much so far. But in terms of applied good suspicion, this question is aimed at pushing us out onto no-man's-land, again. It's meant to jolt us out of our comfortable certainties.

When navigating the torrent of facts and negotiating a host of competing claims to "the real," we need to be aware of how conspiracism works alongside our consumption of the news. Just over the horizon of what we can possibly know, and even in the mediated Disreality of the "now" that comes to us through our preferred platforms and screens, conspiratorial narratives emerge to offer controlled and predictable explanations of events. They tell stories in ways that confirm our original perception by projecting it onto the void of shadowy unknowns.

Conspiratorial narratives can be natural, inherent to our own perception where we connect the dots in patterns that make sense to us. These narratives can also be foreign, exogenous to our own way of seeing things but part of communities of which we consider ourselves to be a part. Trump's claim of election fraud in 2020 worked this way for millions of evangelicals.

Sure, the suspicion of "the left" was present among those whose perception was shaped by "the right." But the story of a Democrat capture of the electoral machinery, along with the provisional "false facts" trotted out in defense of the narrative, was too much for any one person to connect for themselves. This conspiratorial narrative both framed and supercharged the suspicion of millions of Americans.

By asking ourselves, "Why do I want this to be true?" or "Why do I need this to be false?" we practice a good suspicion. One that isn't serving our perceptions but is rather directed against them. And I think this is a distinctly Christian question. At least when we consider Martin Luther's insight that "all of life is conversion." The other word commonly used here instead of "conversion" is "repentance." But I like conversion. It's the translation offered by Swiss theologian Karl Barth, and I think it captures the dynamic part of the Christian life.

Metanoia, or repentance, isn't some mechanical, transactional, single assent to a claim. It is both an original and ongoing disruption of our way of seeing the world, all proceeding from the confession that Jesus is God's Word. This Word cuts us to the quick. Repentance tends to evoke a religious feeling, but not an unsettling. But that is what conversion really is, a dispossession of our claims to certainty. This dispossession ends up delivering us. We are free to consider what we might have otherwise denied or distorted.

This Christian element is precisely why I believe directing suspicion against our perceptions can be an act of faith. And the constant carrying and asking of this question, both in Christian community and of our own selves, can prepare us—help us—to practice good suspicion in a time of so much distortion.

What would I need to unlearn if this isn't true?

Good suspicion recognizes unlearning as a form of learning. This is incredibly costly. And sets us back considerably. But this is what good suspicion does. It is comfortable asking after the stakes of change. It recognizes that the cost of change tends to be lower than the pain of not changing. Especially when the stories we tell become more and more abstract, and more and more in defense of our own perception rather than based on encounter, of both God and our neighbor. This twofold encounter demands we recognize unlearning as the consequence of change.

That's the reason I like this question—it helps shine a light on not just the cost of changing our minds, but also the path we'll need to walk as a consequence of this change. And this can feel so insurmountable to so many of us that we don't bother trying. But we have no other choice. The assumption here though is that this happens overnight. Nothing could be further from the truth. Unlearning takes time. And it takes a community.

Hans Ulrich calls the church the "place of reversal."[12] I like the vision this represents of the church not as a program, but rather an outworking of the unexpected, upside-down kingdom made possible by the life of the crucified Jesus. The resurrection marks a reversal of falsehood and the violence enacted in its defense.

In this sense, the church should be communities of unlearning, where this reversal is recognized and encouraged. The church can be, should be, more of a shock to our senses than it is. But this reversal cannot happen when the unity of the church is grounded in anything less than Jesus. Churches that serve communion from the party platform and not the table of Jesus will go on about "biblical morality" without recognizing that the unity they manufacture isn't the unity created by the broken body of Jesus. How else might we explain the pervasive popularity of "make America great again" and evangelicalism? The unity of evangelicals is no threat to this slogan and its power; in fact, the unity of evangelicals is represented by this slogan.

Too often in America, many churches have so watered down the gospel so as to make it little more than the good news of middle-class respectability. In other churches, doctrinal pedigree is so high up in the lofty clouds that their feet never touch the grit of the pavement. They bypass the plight of the poor or the needs of the marginalized by confusing an awareness and ability to articulate that plight with the sacrifice to alleviate it.

Remember, the churches in America tell a story about America, whether they realize it or not. The telling of this story is varied. As a narrative, this story will—depending on the church—contradict with and clash against other tellings.

And even here, these stories can be told explicitly or through a more insidious silence that leaves the dominant prevailing myths about America untouched.

A great deal of being Christian in America today, I believe, involves the responsibility to both name and unlearn the myths of our nation and the perceptions they curate among us. Christian proclamation, the preaching of the Christian message, doesn't have to take a deft or blind eye to the stories of America. Rather, we take our context and our time seriously by incorporating our moment and the vestiges of our memories and myths into consideration in the act of preaching and ministering the reality of God. But this doesn't end here!

The unlearning I have in mind, the kind contained in this good suspicion, isn't cerebral and intellectual alone. Though it certainly involves that. Yes, we will need a renewed interest in and capacity for learning beyond entertainment. We cannot disparage "do your own research" and then ignore the potential and possibility of platforms to assuage ignorance. But there's a limit to what all this sort of knowledge can do and be.

I once posted an article offering an analysis of some news story. It doesn't matter what it was. What matters is that it was written by a historian, that it was attempting to analyze something in the first weeks of the second Trump administration. And my friend asked, "How can I even begin to understand what's going on? I feel like I have my Bible, my kids, and my life—but that's it. How do I not go frantic but at the same time learn what's going on around me?"

Recognizing we need to unlearn what have been essential elements of our perception demands a community. It takes wider horizons. It takes time. But none of this has to be frantic. None of this has to set us on edge. We don't need to fret about what we don't know. We simply need to rest content in a life of learning, of cultivating awareness, and perhaps of recapturing wonder.

If everything is certain, then you've successfully eliminated wonder along with the chaos of unknowing. While unlearning might daunt us at first, we can acknowledge its great gift. Unlearning can make way for new discovery, putting wonder—that emotional response to the new—back on the table. This horizon of wonder can serve as motivation to step out into the unknown and the uncertainty that our narratives of comfort have tried to protect us from.

Take conspiratorial narratives about immigrants. Let's assume we've bought into the storied claim that every immigrant is a violent criminal. First asking ourselves, "Why do I want every immigrant to be a criminal?" puts us on a path to discover more about the experience of migration because, suddenly, assumptions and desires are out in the open. We forget that on the other side of certainty is often ignorance. On the other side of what appears "clear" or "obvious" is a host of unexamined assumptions. This is why this question matters. Because on the heels of recognizing that our desires are at work in the stories we tell to reinforce our perceptions is its sequel: recognizing we have work to do.

I learned this as a white American in the 2010s. This was my decade of coming to grips with the legacy and histories of race in America. But it's not over with. That's just when I was cognizant that it had begun. That was when I first became aware I was beginning to unlearn my perceptions and encounter different experiences that drew mine out onto the landscape of doubt and uncertainty. And because so much of the evangelical Christianity I knew was tangled up in preserving majority position over others while claiming the minority position on the field of political battles, this encounter provoked a crisis of faith, too.

The deepest forms of unlearning will not only bring us face-to-face with our neighbor. They will inevitably expose the false veneers and distorted attributes we've wrongly applied to God. This matters because so much of the evangelical certainties baked into corrupt suspicion have a theological stake. In unlearning elements of American history, many Christians will also have to unlearn beliefs about the god who they once believed sanctioned this mythologized version of American greatness, too. In unlearning parts of economic theory and detaching it from Christian faith, many Christians will also have to repent from worshipping a god whose Eleventh Commandment was the preservation of unbridled capitalism.

Unlearning is learning. And the work of reexamining

the assumptions that enclose our perception is painful, disorienting, and not something we usually choose willingly. But when we realize the domino effect in our unlearning, we can better name and also navigate the path that faith walks. We can recognize that a life of learning isn't confined to educational institutions or the special call of academics. In asking what we might have to unlearn if the assumptions and narratives we project on the world are found to be untrue or unstable, then we practice critical living, not mere thinking.

Remember, if all of the Christian life is conversion, then we never "arrive" at some controlled worldview that enables us to see reality in totality—that's what ideology offers. No, the church is always and ever on the move—learning, repenting, dying, and rising again. I like how the German pastor theologian Ernst Käsemann puts it. Käsemann was a pastor who voted for Hitler in 1933. Decades later, he wrote the following words in an essay titled "What I, as a German Theologian, Unlearned in Fifty Years."

> Christian faith is not thinkable without that exodus in which Abraham turned his back on his father's house and his friends. It is doubtful whether life can be fruitful if it is not prepared to be in rebellion against old tradition and traditional privileges, if it is not prepared resolutely to throw off ballast where new horizons are to be won.[13]

Unlearning as a dimension of good suspicion isn't meeting ossified conservatism with the blind zeal of progressivism. It is about recognizing unlearning as a healthy part of the Christian life.

Who do I need to encounter?

Good suspicion invites others to shape our perception through encounter. I believe the church can be the site for this encounter, but it doesn't have to be exclusive. We encounter one another in so many different ways. But good suspicion takes this a step further by seeking out encounters by participation and involvement in common, collaborative ventures.

I'm not talking about arbitrary, performative meet and greets. I'm talking about a way of life that makes the encountering of difference a daily occurrence. This comes, I think, by taking on responsibility and the offering of hospitality. Whether through common ventures such as local governance or community service or through common meals, the potential for true human encounter is made possible. It entails the recognition that the material infrastructure of American life is itself a barrier to the sort of diversity and difference that the church itself is equipped to recognize, elevate, and celebrate as a sign of the rule of Jesus operating in its midst.

And if corrupted suspicion affirms our perception over and against another, then good suspicion enables us to truly and authentically encounter another person with open hands and an open mind.

This doesn't have to degenerate into an undetermined, free-floating, secular no-man's-land that combines all forms of difference into a static experience of sameness so that, ironically, difference and diversity are destroyed. No, what I mean is that the freedom to really encounter people is part of what good suspicion welcomes.

But this is challenging simply by how our social world is constructed and determined by our physical and digital spaces. We come to assume things about others before we ever encounter them. None of us are the caricatures our enemies create. We are complex. Whitman is right, we contain multitudes. And how easy it is to not only forget this, but to live in a state of willed ignorance.

One of the oddest experiences of my life was moving back to America after three years abroad. While three years doesn't seem like much, it was enough for seemingly normal aspects of American life to become other and uncanny. I'm not sure we Americans realize how much our subdivisions, our urbanization, our chaotic ordering of physical space impacts our relational capacity, our awareness of people "unlike us," and our ability to connect across difference, in the negative. Simply put, I wonder if, looking back, a great many people didn't come to the megachurch I served at in the Bible Belt because our grass was cut too nice.

This isn't just me talking about middle-class respectability, food deserts, lack of reliable transportation, or the odd, immense reliance on cars (and the infrastructure that demands). This is also me recognizing that the history of infrastructure in America is deeply shaped (and so permanently scarred) by our unresolved racism. Whether by redlining or carceral police practices, the story of America is given a permanent witness in and by the shape of our communities.

Tragically, Helen Kenyon's observation back in 1952 that 11 a.m. on Sunday remains the most segregated hour in America continues to be true.[14] And this isn't just true of segregation of ethnicities, but classes, too. And what's more, churches in America have, by and large, been subjected to this development and have, among evangelicals, been active architects in its construction.

When I was a pastor in Virginia, I was encouraged to grow my college ministry by what was called the homogeneous unit principle (HUP). It was the prevailing strategy of something called the church growth movement, which was incredibly popular in the 1970s and '80s into the '90s. It was taught in many if not most evangelical seminaries.

The HUP was based on missionary research conducted by Donald McGavran in the 1940s and '50s among the caste society of India. McGavran found that Indians converted to Christianity at a higher rate so long as they converted into communities that reinforced the caste system. His colleague C. Peter Wagner founded the Church Growth Institute at

Fuller Theological Seminary in California and expanded McGavran's work into twentieth-century America.

As you can imagine, to white evangelicals struggling to retain the old ways in the aftermath of civil rights, the homogeneous unit principle gave them the dataset they needed to promote their prejudiced understanding of "God's design" and "created order." While Wagner and McGavran kept claiming the homogeneous unit principle was not a license for white supremacy,[15] the marketing of their Church Growth techniques betrayed these claims. A back cover endorsement of Wagner's hit book read,

> *Our Kind of People* attacks the Christian guilt complex arising from the civil rights movement and puts it to rest with a skillful mixture of scriptural precedent and human psychology. In doing so, Wagner transforms the statement that "11 a.m. on Sunday is the most segregated hour in America" from a millstone around Christian necks into a dynamic tool for assuring Christian growth.[16]

I share this historical anecdote here because to practice good suspicion and ask, "Who do I need to encounter?" in modern America will involve some work beyond words. While McGavran would continue to speak against white supremacy, the simple fact is that the reception of his work in the hands of functional white supremacists—those who disavow personal racism but practice its structural forms—leads me to conclude that encountering one another across difference is the practice of good suspicion.

In asking, "Who do I need to encounter?" we open our perception up to the shared experiences of others. All the intellectual arguments in the world, all the histories of unlearning, none of that will prepare you for the ruining that comes from finding out those who were targeted as your enemy were not what they said they were.

More than you or I probably realize. Asking this question involves making material decisions and commitments. Encounter means altering the shape of your life and mine. It means seeking out community and building community that exists both aware of divisions and across them. The simple truth is that our churches, our physical communities, and through algorithms—our digital ones, too—are all shaped by commitments to sameness and controlled encounter. To get practical, taking on the responsibility of volunteer work—like coaching your kid's youth soccer team or serving at a nonprofit hospice organization in your community—will put you in positions where encounter is beyond the influence of the normative design of American life.

And to the degree that these communities shape our perception of "people like us," we need to find escape vectors out of their constricting, limiting holds on our imagination and interaction. The early church was so scandalous precisely in its willingness to gather across seemingly impenetrable social barriers. Ever since State Christianity became the tool of Empire, it has been about the maintenance of imperial borders, not the service of the table of Christ.

Good suspicion recognizes that to encounter another is to encounter Christ. That is, because Jesus identifies with human, every human being images Jesus to us. There's a common belief, widely held, that everyone is made "in the image of God." This is language from Genesis. Theologian Brian Brock helped me understand that it is Jesus's solidarity with humanity that deepens the idea of "Made in the image of God" into "This person is Christ to me."

What if all humanity, in all our differences and disabilities, is represented in and by Jesus Christ? If Jesus is the "first born" from the dead, the one in whom all humanity's hope rests according to the Christian faith, then to say that Jesus is the image of God is to suggest that he stands in solidarity with all humanity. This means, shockingly, not just that each human has dignity, but that every human's destiny is bound up in Jesus's work on their behalf. Jesus takes up in himself the whole and the individual parts of our humanity.

No human being we meet is without dignity or value. Because every human being is given a future in God. This is true of you, me, and those seemingly lost to the pull of conspiracism. We never encounter someone who isn't, in some way, shape, or form, represented by Jesus to God and thus represents Jesus to us. The implications of this truth are vast. But for us in Disreality, I believe it means we are delivered from the illusion that we can persuade or coerce anyone out of conspiracism head-on. This doesn't mean we are silent when it comes to consequential conversations or claims; it means that we never lose sight of the human being.

THE WORLD OF SHADOW AND A WORLD IN COMMON

In 1942, a small group of Nazi officials gathered in the German suburb of Wannsee for a conference. Over the course of a single day, these men laid the logistical groundwork to carry out the transportation and execution of six million people. The atrocities perpetrated in the Holocaust or *shoah* began in human hearts—and in a business meeting.

Good suspicion admits there is much we do not know, and cannot know. It recognizes that truth is slow, and that evil is real. And yet it boldly entrusts all it does not know and cannot know to the prevailing ability of truth to win out in ways that often defy our ability to predict or control.

In the case of the Wannsee conference, the conference organizers conspired to hide the truth of what transpired that day, editing minutes and creating a false record. As the war drew to a close, all surviving minutes were destroyed, save one—that of Undersecretary Martin Luther. This surviving copy led to arrests, prosecutions, and executions.

Good suspicion in a world of shadow is a dangerous way

to live. It doesn't embrace naivety, a head-in-the-sand escapism or piety. No, it knows that there is much that cannot be known, that transpires beyond what we can possibly see or understand, or—most importantly—beyond what we can control.

And in a world of deepfakes, of artificial intelligences that can render videos and content that seem to fracture the very ground on which we stand, good suspicion grows comfortable with saying "I don't know" while, at the same time, daring to act for the good of others nearest our own concrete lives. This combination of humility with honest action runs counter to the zealous certainty that drives the authoritarian.

In an age of highly processed information and authoritarian propaganda, perhaps the way forward toward truth is to once again mark out our limits, to courageously refuse to encounter someone through the suspicions and stories that come to us through digital mediation. Good suspicion is how we learn to tell the truth again in a time of Disreality.

Delivered from our totalities, suspicion becomes something leveled against ourselves and not others. We become aware, painfully so, of how totality shapes perception to make us suspect anyone other than ourselves.

The reality of God makes it possible to talk about good suspicion, the kind directed back on our own selves, our totalities and their securities. This good suspicion makes a common world possible in a world of shadows, even and perhaps especially for those who do not count themselves as followers of Jesus.

Good suspicion in and among the churches makes for hospitality, rather than hostility. It is, in so many words, to prepare ourselves to offer cups of water to Christ on the street, to visit Christ in prison, to sit with Christ on death row, because Christ is the image of God, the first human whose life has become "the light of humanity" (John 1). It is hard to cave to the pull of conspiracism when the human being across from you is treated as Christ himself.

Chapter 8

SAND IN THE MACHINE

> **So let us pick up
> the stones over which we stumble,
> friends, and build altars.**
>
> —Pádraig Ó Tuama, "Oremus"

Disreality throws us back on the most primal of questions: What is reality? And, how should we live? Contained in the stories that answer these questions are visions of our shared existence, of what we have in common, and how we go on, together.

And it is right here where the Christian faith offers itself to the world. Not just as some abstract answer or rationality, but as a life, as a welcome to the suspicious, the cynical, the skeptic, to everyone. The life of Jesus bids us to live this perilous pilgrimage in mystery together, or sulk back into totality, its illusions of certainty, and forms of coercion. This is a dead end.

APOSTASY, NOW

Conspiracy theory has always been a load-bearing wall in the house of evangelical Christianity in America. And pressed into service of aspiring authoritarianism, this Christianity betrays itself by bending the knee to truth established by violence. Evangelicalism has promoted and protected this totality for too long.

In a host of variations, conspiracy theory works inside this evangelicalism as a storytelling act. It performs this task in tandem with a disoriented Christian story, lending urgency, credibility, or relevancy to the gospel evangelicals have come to offer America. The conspiratorial gospel worships a paranoiac Jesus, who sanctions myths of America as part of the Christian story itself.

This gospel has been framed as a conspiracy-busting force and as authority for conspiratorial claims themselves. The entanglement of conspiracism with evangelicalism is so intimate, so inherent that it merely reflects the paranoid Christ at its very center. Who is Jesus but a Christian and a white American? The totality of holy paranoia cannot see or say anything other than this.

This mixed image of Jesus is enough to fuel not just a crisis of fact, but also a crisis of faith that lies at the very center of the totality of holy paranoia. But nobody needs a PhD to recognize this.

A glance around the ruins of reality is enough.

The pain is obvious. It lives in silences kept between family members; it operates in the fissures that divide churches and communities. And whether you have ever been to an evangelical church or attended an evangelical school, the influence of evangelical Christianity on America means that you have a stake in this problem in one form or another.

Conspiratorial thinking in American evangelicalism isn't a bug, but rather a feature of its own unique totality. It's a totality that evolved across American history, taking shape through interacting with specific anxieties and uncertainties in every period, from women's bodies and witchcraft to revolts that upturned the system of chattel slavery all the way to today's right-wing deep-state fears. The stakes involved in telling the truth are serious, as is the cost when that task is ignored by Christians.

The cost isn't primarily conceptual, but concrete. Human lives and human existence itself are altered by the words we speak and the world created by these rogue words. The cost and consequence of totality is measured not by lack of factual evidence alone but also in the practice of falsehood that leads to eradication and erasure of human lives. To inhabit totality is to practice falsehood: to promote truth established by violence.

Whether or not evangelicals recognize this history isn't the point. Responsibility is.

Here at the end, I won't issue a call to reform or repair or resurrect evangelicalism. Having walked the way myself, I have come to recognize what I can only understand as the making of apostasy from the ways of knowing that have come to characterize not just this community, but the confession of Jesus it makes.

Because the totality of holy paranoia is both inherited and inhabited, the ruin of this totality can only be described as apostasy. And I believe this can be a step of faith.

After all, this is the sort of liberating faith the Scriptures have always witnessed to. From Abraham stepping out of his father's house into an unknown land, to the exodus out from under the imperial machine of Pharaoh, faith is always and ever a liberating apostasy from false securities and perilous certainties.

To speak this way is to speak in the grammar and logic of story. Not just raw fact, but by a story that promotes and provokes attention to specific facts, namely God's acts of deliverance across history with his people.

Yes, we should call our common citizens and fellow human beings to facts, but truth-telling is always *more* than the facts. Truth-telling factors in the central question: How should we live? We can weigh facts as presented by scientific inquiry, academic consensus, and the like. But the power of story is in its ability to offer an answer to the sort of life we ought to live. The facts by themselves cannot do this.

A time for Disreality calls for better facts *and* better story. And this implicates all of us who live in the ruins of reality but long for a better world.

SAND IN THE MACHINERY

The resistance in World War II used the phrase "sand in the machine" to describe their subversive mission to disrupt European fascism from the inside. This phrase captures much of what this book has been attempting to do with evangelicalism and America in view.

By telling the untold history of evangelicalism and its affinity for conspiracy theory, I'm trying to throw sand in the machinery that gives plausibility to so many conspiracist claims about America and our place in it. And you can, too.

We throw sand in the machinery of holy paranoia every time we answer conspiracy theory with the question "Why do you want this to be true?" Every time we challenge what passes as "the facts" by looking at the stories that sort and interpret them, we throw sand in the machinery and live out the implications of good suspicion.

Good suspicion prepares us for good resistance, for tossing sand in the machinery of totality. It is a resistance defined by two main elements: uncertainty and subversion.

Understanding how early worshippers of Jesus Christ came to be called "Christians" and then to claim it for themselves gives us some insight into how we can describe ourselves in terms of uncertainty and subversion without giving ourselves over to the sort of violent militancy that erupted on January 6.

Millennia ago, in the political world of the Roman Empire, partisan identity was signaled by an "-iani" suffix. Sort of like how "-crat" or "-can" works for Democrat and Republican. So there were Herodiani, partisans of King Herod, there were Augustiani, partisans of Caesar, and—suddenly in Antioch—there were Christiani.

"Christian" wasn't originally a name created by the churches for the churches. It wasn't branding. It was a label applied to a group of people by the prevailing political culture to code them in terms of partisan politics. And the coding was dangerous.

To be coded in partisan terms as a Christiani meant you identified politically and socially with either a backwater mystery cult or an insurrectionary movement against Rome—the jury was still out. The point was, you were different. This was a collective label, not an individual one.

This label communicated political subversion, defiance, and dissent. But that coding was also a way to bring the mysterious into certain understandable categories.

How else were outsiders to understand this group of people who defied social norms and seemed to worship an executed Jew, whose central belief was encapsulated in a political subversive challenge to Caesar, "Jesus is Lord"? In that time, Lord was Caesar's title, and nobody else's.

This social context is what frames Peter's instructions to the churches in his letter where he writes, "If any of you suffer as a Christiani, don't be ashamed but glorify God in that name" (1 Peter 4:16). And so it became common for the earliest worshippers of Jesus to claim the name assigned to them by the prevailing political order.

They didn't have to do that. They could have contended with it. Resisted it. They could have parsed it, pacified it, made it palatable to Roman sensibilities, but they didn't.

Their embrace of a label meant to code them as dangerous signaled in many ways a primal dissent from the power claims of the Roman Empire rooted in a theological confession: Jesus is Lord. It signaled the Christian community's understanding that "the old has gone, and the new is on its way"—and this meant the Roman claim to total authority was arbitary; this meant too that those who lived on the margins of Roman power were now in the very place where God's Kingdom was made visible.

But all this lost its edge once Christianity became the State religion. As heirs to this long, tired legacy, we've lost what Willie Jennings calls the "real criminality" associated with Christian teaching and our preaching.[1] In the Rome of antiquity, the subversive, criminal quality of faith was pushed out into the margins and the monasteries.

Now look around America. The question of what it means

to be Christian is given answers that cannot be reconciled. We cannot walk the way of totality and receive God's reality.

Both an acceptance of uncertainty and peaceful subversiveness mark the way of God's reality. Together, these qualities flesh out what it means to be faithful dissidents to Jesus Christ in an age of disinformation, those in whom good suspicion is a posture, and discipleship is the path. And that means responsibility, one step at a time.

A LIGHT TO OUR PATH

I grew up in Tampa Bay—this incredible place where manatees lazily float between mangroves under a vast blue sky and massive bridges, connecting all these spits of development emerging up from the old, wild Florida. I rode across these bridges almost every day. Each lined with streetlights pushing back the tropical darkness.

But when I moved to Virginia, night driving was something else entirely. Unlike in St. Pete, streetlights were hard to find. I was a much slower driver those first few months in Virginia.

But after I got over the shock of Virginia country driving at night, I decided to do something stupid. When I'd get on a straightaway, without any cars behind or in front, I'd switch off my headlights. Darkness enveloped. It was startling. But also thrilling. Darkness that you couldn't find if you were looking for it back in Tampa Bay. And I'd see how long I could drive before enough terror told me to turn the lights back on.

I memorized this verse as a kid: "Your Word is a lamp to my feet, and a light to my path" (Psalm 119:105). And it's only these past few years that I've come to recognize how wrong I got this verse. I got it wrong because my imagination was at home in Tampa Bay, and not Virginia backroads.

I used to think of this verse as sort of promising me the whole picture. Not unlike how conspiracy theories function as applied theology, giving us the "full picture" that God "promises" us as Christians. The problem is: God doesn't.

A "lamp to our feet" is the smallest sort of light source imaginable. It casts light for our next step, and that's enough. As God's Word to us, Jesus doesn't illuminate the whole map of discipleship. Our way through the world as dissidents isn't clearly marked—it's carefully discerned one step at a time.

This shift in how we imagine the vocation of dissident discipleship introduces us to something essential to the whole endeavor of faith: uncertainty.

UNCERTAINTY AT THE HEART OF THINGS

In the field of quantum physics, there's something known as Heisenberg's uncertainty principle. Imagine you have a tiny bouncy ball. This ball represents an electron, one of the fundamental building blocks of matter. You toss this electron ball back and forth between your hands and decide you want to measure how fast it's moving at the halfway point.

Heisenberg tells us that, at the quantum level, there's a fundamental limit to how precisely we can know both an electron's position and its momentum at the same time. The more accurately we determine where the electron is, the less precisely we can know how fast it's moving—and vice versa. This isn't just a limitation of our tools; it's a fundamental property of nature. Uncertainty is built into bare reality.

And Jesus teaches something similar for the reality of God. The gospel of John records a nighttime encounter between Nicodemus, a teacher of Israel, and Jesus. Nicodemus stumbling forward into the radical, inbreaking reality of God. "How can these things be?" he asks. Jesus's teachings seemed to simultaneously fulfill and upend all he thought he knew. "The wind blows where it wishes," Jesus tells him, "and you cannot tell where it is coming from, and where it is going. This is how it is with everyone who lives by the Spirit."[2]

Uncertainty is an uncomfortable mark of discipleship. Christians need to be reminded of this again in an age of (dis)information. As the speed and volume of information has everyone grasping for certainty and security, Christian faith initiates people into a way of knowing that is comfortable with, even defined by, uncertainty. It establishes the sharpest of contrasts with conspiracies and myths of history, stories that become totalities, constructing a facade of certainty only for it to crumble in the next chaotic, unexplainable event.

It shouldn't strike us as strange that "static" and "status quo" emerge from the same root idea: stability. But stability of what? Discipleship in the way of Jesus, in his own words, is picking up a Cross. That act, that imagery, was sand in the machinery of the Roman Empire and the grip it held on the Mediterranean. The Cross as a symbol of liberation wasn't just odd, it was incredible—as in, it lacked any sort of credibility to the idea of freedom and salvation.

But this vocation, the Cruciform life, is actually shown to be credible in the crucible of human chaos because it offers peaceable truth in a time when many confuse order with truth, and establish it by a sword. The Cross isn't an invitation to conquest, to truth by violence. The Cross is initiation into a life that is itself a Word that renews the world. It is a truth made viable and has veracity exclusively in the resurrection of Jesus.

Anyone can suggest "Christians should tell the truth" or promote various forms of media literacy. This can be moralizing; it can also be practical wisdom. But it is another thing to suggest that truth-telling as Christians is inseparable from the way, the truth, and the life of Jesus, and to consider the shape of truth-telling as a witness to a crucified life. This life, a crucified and risen life, exposes and disrupts the cycle of falsehood and violence, of truth by power.

Discipleship in this way of the Cross enacts a sabotage of all we take for granted and assume as given, especially what counts as "biblical" or "faithful." Between books, podcasts, conferences, and celebrity influencers, Christians have come to think of discipleship in America as a set of techniques to be mastered. As a dataset to be amassed. And we are constantly introduced to these techniques by a diet of content we consume. Here, the only problem isn't what we know, but how we apply it. That sense of mastery is dangerous.

Dissident discipleship isn't a passive consumption or accumulation of spiritual principles. Discipleship involves an active dispossession that normalizes uncertainty. If discipleship is training, it is a training in a life that, when pressed, says along with Jesus, human beings "do not live by bread alone, but by every word that comes from the Father." Dissident discipleship, then, keeps us in an active posture of listening for the divine Word. It is anchored in relationship, rather than might and dominion. The uncertainty that is the mark of disciples to Jesus is one deeply aware of our own ongoing re-cognition according to the story of Jesus. This means we must remain uncertain, stubbornly so, in the face of those who try to convince us that human beings deemed "illegal" can be denied the dignity of rights and mercy. We must remain uncertain in a way that provokes action.

When Jesus quoted this Scripture about bread in the wilderness, he was rehearsing and resolving Israel's own failure to live in the midst of uncertainty, to rely on the provision of God after being liberated from slavery and empire in Egypt. Discipleship in this way of living, this way of the faith, is deeply unsettling because it subverts our inherited and reflexive ways of narrating the world around us.

In so many ways, conspiracy theories in the hands of Christians are powerful stories of self-justification, the stones we turn into bread to survive in the wilderness. They point away from ourselves and shift the blame onto the nefarious, shadowy "them." The certainty these stories curate is as predictable as it is potent in the political.

Rather than coercively lording the Ten Commandments over the American populace in public spaces, Christians in America must encounter the God who delivers us in the very space of common good that these commands mark out. Have we loved God and neighbor? No amount of coercive moralizing can make up for neglect that refuses responsibility.

With one eye on the commands, and another on Disreality, we find Christian faith provokes uncertainty in all of the slogans, all the memes, all the content that would render reality a certain way. The totalities that we inhabit, and that conspiracy theory works to preserve, are adept at short-circuiting encounters without our neighbor. We cannot trust conspiracism to set our neighbor in front of us.

But to the extent that our lives are shaped by material affluence, technological convenience, and militant dominance—to the extent that these weave together a life we call "normal" and protect as "given"—we will struggle to embrace the unsettling uncertainty that is the mark of Christian witness to and solidarity with a world loved by, and reconciled in, God's reality. Even if it denies it. Especially so.

UNCERTAINTY HERE AND NOW

The discipleship industry, that host of books, conferences, and podcasts, presents the idea that discipleship is merely the sum total of spiritual techniques, a one-size-fits-all for all times and places. This industry discounts how each time and place contains its own unique set of challenges. Faithfulness in our time is faithfulness in our time.

We can openly name that dissident discipleship is an uncertain endeavor, as it honestly faces the concrete, real, and lived challenges and winds of change of its time.

The uncertainty of discipleship requires courage, not just character. And this courage is Christian when we act and so live in the confidence of God's command for our context. We cannot discount that the novel element of our time involves the speed and volume of information. We cannot expect discipleship to move past, unaware that the emergence of conspiracism alters and distorts the Christian story in our churches.

Because of the power of holy paranoia to fracture not only Christian community but also political community, the radical uncertainty will make some startling claims in this moment that draws our attention back to God's kingdom. All the suspicion leveled against LGBTQ+ people, all the scapegoating in the name of "woke" and DEI, all the preemptive denial of a ravaged climate—the result of our greedy hands that exploit the natural world while quoting Genesis about "exercising dominion." This exploitative dominance is a denial of God because the greed that strips the world of its resources does so by exploiting the labor of human beings. This sort of uncertainty—applied to common, pressing issues—enables a fresh consideration of supposedly settled questions.

Christianity has always been intimate with paradox. The existential eruption of Jesus's life among Christians is as spontaneous as it is surprising. What makes discipleship so uncertain becomes clearer the more we recognize discipleship isn't a system, but a directive, one that involves a responsible, active courage that, in its acting, makes visible a particular character, a particular life: the life of Jesus Christ. And it is the life that comes to us in those we encounter. But rendered by totality, we miss the manifold ways Jesus comes to us every day.

Christians should expect to recognize and narrate our lives by the contours of the story we claim is at the heart of all human striving and existence. We should come to expect, then, that our lives find greater and greater resonance not only to the joys that mark the people of God but also to the suffering and misunderstanding that characterizes the scandal of the gospel, not conspiracy.

DISSIDENT SUBVERSION

There is also subversion at the heart of Christian apostasy. If the goal of propaganda is to normalize and legitimize the ruling powers in their actions, Christianity injects subversive uncertainty at the heart of things. Good suspicion is how this uncertainty is revealed without corrupting our common life, but holds open the possibility of introducing changes toward justice and mercy.

By refusing to accept any and all totalities as placeholders for "reality," dissident disciples become practitioners of good suspicion—this is the suspicion the world needs. This suspicion builds. Because it is marked by a confidence that God's reality sustains the world. This is empowering, and not cause for evacuation. Good suspicion takes seriously God's promise to sustain human life without recourse to violence and its conceptual forms like hierarchy, patriarchy, and white supremacy.

Delivered from the need to establish truth through violence, dissident disciples become people who are radically free to consider facts and truth. This weighing of facts occurs not as isolated autonomous individuals endowed with the power of rationality, but as participants in a discerning, worshipping community that is deeply enmeshed in the common life of the world—creatively, locally, and responsibly, protesting the intrusive and coercive powers of our time, be they old tyrannies or new terrors. This subversive vision of dissident discipleship, as communal as it is uncertain, throws sand in the machinery of holy paranoia that rages in our public life. It does this courageously, refusing to go along with supposed certainties and the violence that enacts them, while remaining deeply committed to a way of living together that depicts what human life for one another before God can be.

A WORLD IN COMMON

Because Christianity announces the reconciliation of the world to God, those formed by the Christian story are ready to anticipate in word and work the common world we share. This is no utopian dream. This is the work of witness and the call to participate in what God is already doing: repairing the ruins of our common world.

Good suspicion forms us into the sort of people who are fit to bear with those lost to the conspiratorial void. Good suspicion empowers us with facts, yes, but most importantly with the epistemic humility that knows the pain involved in having our own totalities and certainties sabotaged. The friends, family, or community lost to conspiracism aren't reached in the blinding light of enlightenment, but in the patient endurance of stubborn, relentless confidence that the truth will have its day.

So the difference lies in whether we become a people who claim to possess the truth, or people claimed by the truth, such that the Christian faith has always articulated.

FINDING A WAY FORWARD

As you survey the ruins in which we live, I want to leave you with a word of hope—even if it can't be a single answer or a solution that fixes everything wrong in Disreality.

Much of the pain and crisis of conspiracism we feel is personal, though we see its chaos more broadly. But Jesus, I think, meets us in the personal first. The point where God enters our pain and human situation becomes the site of sacred encounter.

The scandal of Jesus's ministry was felt first and with the most force in his hometown. After a controversial healing in his local synagogue, his mother and brothers attempted to cut through the crowd to get to Jesus. "Your family is looking for you," came the message. Jesus's response is often interpreted as a gentle rebuke to his family, but it also expresses a word of hope to those who know the pain and loss on the pilgrimage of faith. Jesus asked, "Who are my mother and my brothers?" and then said something startling for its newness: "Whoever does the will of God is my brother and sister and mother."³

You may not be able to argue facts successfully, but we can and we must tell the truth that is more than facts, but never less. We can do this in the hope that this truth-telling makes a future possible, and unites a community right now in the midst of so much loss.

It isn't the sum total of facts and figures and data alone that counts. What counts is better stories. The future we hope for and can build out of Disreality will demand such stories, and people of humility rather than violence. And that future begins with a decision to recognize truth in all its forms.

This decision sets us on a course away from the illusions of certainties contained in holy paranoia. To be swept up in Jesus's words "I am the way, the truth, and the life"⁴ does not grant omniscience, does not sanction Christian authority in the political, does not endorse totality and its violence. It sets us free, on a perilous pilgrimage, where saying "I don't know" and asking ourselves, "Why do I want this to be true?" keeps us attentive and receptive to God's reality that is being revealed in the human beings around us. The story of God is bigger than us, it does not depend on us, and it encompasses the world in a more expansive care than we might ever imagine. We might live amid the ruins now, but God is actively and presently working toward renewal, and in this we dissident disciples might anchor our hope.

Apostasy from holy paranoia is an act of faith. And this faith, though it passes the borders patrolled by evangelicalism, can live in and for a common world loved and sustained by God. Whatever becomes of evangelicalism, our lives are too short to deny God's liberation by defending broken and malformed tradition.

God's reality and its liberation have created a processional across history, a people renewed as dissident disciples: creative, local, and responsible witnesses to the story of common world renewal. This truth initiates a subversion of the world's violence it wraps in falsehoods because at the Cross, the death of truth does not destroy reality but renews it.

Reality *is* in ruins. The common world we once assumed and took for granted is gone. And to be a people of the truth means tapping into our emotional register, not only our rational one. This means we must lament, mourn, cry out. Lament the ruins, and the distorting dehumanization taking place around us. Even though I suppose we've forgotten how to do this—do it imperfectly, do it in faith that God makes much of our groaning. Give voice to regret, to pain, to loss. The prophets of the Scriptures can give us the words. "He has made me dwell in darkness," wrote Jeremiah, "like those long dead" (Lamentations 3:6). The pain, the cost, all of what Disreality has wrought in our time is worthy of our lament and righteous anger.

It did not have to be this way. Words charged by holy paranoia built the worlds of harm that—right now—cast their shadow over the ruins we find ourselves in. But even here, we are faced—all of us—with a choice. We can say yes to the call and the responsibility to become people of a better story, beyond the ruining of the conspiratorial gospel. We can fight for a future in which truth is good news for all people, in which human flourishing and justice and equity are enjoyed by all, and not just those deemed "on the right side" of the lesser stories we tell.

So long as the story of Jesus is centered on the crucified, it remains a story of mystery as well as power. How can such a story bring about victory? Conspiracy is endlessly suspicious of others, but at the Cross we grow suspicious of ourselves—our proclivities to power, to violence that promotes falsehood. To be a people of the truth is to be a people in whom good suspicion becomes a way of life. Let us double down on the uncertainty that makes a common world possible. This uncertainty checks our reactivities, our anxieties, our rushing to judgment, and makes way for the reality of God, whose judgment issues in love and reconciliation and human flourishing.

Dissident disciples can never forget the link between this truth and trust. Telling the truth is a courageous act that demands trust, too. Trust that what is true, even if it seems to falter or fail, will always have its day. And for the Christian, trust is (ultimately) a trust in God's reality, God's story.

This trust issues not just in confession, but in a common existence that is in and of itself resistance to the old tyrannies and new terrors of our time. These tyrannies and terrors cannot abide the reality of Jesus, because in their endless drive to establish what is truth through power and violence, the reality of Jesus stands unchanged, and sure. This reality is not something we enforce, but something we receive. The reality of Jesus brings with it the sort of faithful confidence that expresses itself in an uncertainty that itself is dangerous to the authoritarian, to those whose certainty has been weaponized to demonize others.

Are we ready to embark on this existence for the good of those who find themselves rendered by the stories of holy paranoia? Can we resist Christianities that promote harm over healing? We must. We do this all by embracing a responsibility to tell the truth even as we are claimed *by* this very truth ourselves. This truth-telling is willing to admit that it does not possess the truth as much as it is a participant in the truth. This participation is always open to being unsettled, to being corrected, to being conformed to the life of the Crucified whose Word builds a better world, and tells a better story of the liberation of that same world.

The future belongs to this better story of God's reality. And this story makes a common world possible. Can we live in this story now? I believe we can. This choice, this conversion, this decision, grows from a recognition that this story, this God, empowers even the very notion of what is possible. But this is a dangerous way to live. This life is not without cost. New terrors and old tyrannies promise a world of order and oppression. But the common world promised by God will not appear overnight, nor is it made visible without faith. Reality may be in ruins, but the promises of God endure. Such people who find themselves claimed by this truth will also find themselves able to live honestly and responsibily for the good of others in the ruins of reality.

ACKNOWLEDGMENTS

I want to begin by thanking my late high-school English teacher, Lance Lipham. Even if you were here to see it, you wouldn't believe it. Thank you.

A massive thanks to the community and my colleagues at the University of Aberdeen. To Brian Brock and Tom Greggs, thank you for your support, encouragement, and supervision. To Philip Ziegler and Hans Ulrich, thank you for your attention to and engagement with my work. To friends and dialogue partners: Cody Bivins-Starr and Daniel Rempel, thank you for your constant support and timely, critical encouragement. To Andy Hayes and Robbie Dawson, thank you for the gift of your presence. To my agent, Morgan Strehlow, who has fought for this project and believes in the work, thank you! To my editor, Stephanie Smith, thank you for seeing what I could not.

To Mom, Dad, Kevin, and my in-laws, thank you for proving in countless ways that family matters. To the kids, I hope you know I love our time together more than the work this book represents. Remember "the blesseds" and you will always be found by God.

NOTES

Introduction

1. PRRI, "The Persistence of QAnon in the Post-Trump Era: An Analysis of Who Believes the Conspiracies," *PRRI* (blog), accessed February 22, 2023, https://www.prri.org/research/the-persistence-of-qanon-in-the-post-trump-era-an-analysis-of-who-believes-the-conspiracies/.
2. Sophia Moskalenko et al., "Secondhand Conspiracy Theories: The Social, Emotional and Political Tolls on Loved Ones of QAnon Followers," *Democracy and Security* 19, no. 3 (July 3, 2023): 231–50, https://doi.org/10.1080/17419166.2022.2111305.
3. Friedrich Nietzsche, *Thus Spake Zarathustra* (Function), Loc. 1933, Kindle.

Chapter 1: Pain, Panic, and Power

1. Karen M. Douglas and Robbie M. Sutton, "What Are Conspiracy Theories? A Definitional Approach to Their Correlates, Consequences, and Communication," *Annual Review of Psychology* 74, no. 1 (January 4, 2023): 271–98, https://doi.org/10.1146/annurev-psych-032420-031329.
2. "Select Committee to Investigate the January 6th Attack on the United States Capitol," Washington, DC, July 27, 2021.
3. Moskalenko et al., "Secondhand Conspiracy Theories."

4. Sex trafficking is a scourge, after all.
5. Inga Trauthig et al., "The Future of Conspiracy Theory Scholarship," *Journal of Information Technology & Politics* (April 14, 2025): 1–12, https://doi.org/10.1080/19331681.2025.2491687.
6. Richard Ellman, *James Joyce*, new and revised edition (Oxford: Oxford University Press, 1983), 505.
7. PRRI, "The Persistence of QAnon in the Post-Trump Era."
8. William Brand, Columbine—Tragedy and Recovery," *Denver Post* Online, April 28, 1999, https://extras.denverpost.com/news/shot0428m.htm, and Sean Kelly, "Bernalls Defend Book's Accuracy," *Denver Post* Online, September 26, 1999, https://extras.denverpost.com/news/shot0926a.htm.
9. Alissa Wilkinson, "After Columbine, Martyrdom Became a Powerful Fantasy for Christian Teenagers," *Vox*, April 20, 2017, https://www.vox.com/culture/2017/4/20/15369442/columbine-anniversary-cassie-bernall-rachel-scott-martyrdom.
10. Randa Abdel-Fattah, *Coming of Age in the War on Terror* (Sydney: New South Publishing, 2021), 67.
11. Erik Eckholm, "From Right, a Rain of Anti-Clinton Salvos," *New York Times*, June 26, 1994, sec. U.S., https://www.nytimes.com/1994/06/26/us/from-right-a-rain-of-anti-clinton-salvos.html.
12. Irenaeus of Lyon, "Against Heresies" (Book 1, Preface).

Chapter 2: Power of Story

1. Rebecca West, *Black Lamb and Grey Falcon*, reprint edition (New York: Penguin Classics, 2007), 255.
2. Richard Buckminster Fuller and Kiyoshi Kuromiya, *Critical Path* (New York: St. Martin's Press, 1981).
3. Jacques Ellul, *Propaganda: The Formation of Men's Attitudes* (New York: Knopf Doubleday Publishing Group, 1973), xv.
4. Hannah Arendt, *The Origins of Totalitarianism*, 6th ed. (New York: Meridian Books, 1951).
5. Charlie Warzel, "I'm Running Out of Ways to Explain How Bad This Is," *The Atlantic*, October 10, 2024, https://www.theatlantic.com/technology/archive/2024/10/hurricane-milton-conspiracies-misinformation/680221/.

6. Giorgio Agamben. *Homo Sacer: Sovereign Power and Bare Life* (Nachdr. Meridian. Stanford University Press, 2010).
7. Jeff Sharlet, *The Undertow: Scenes from a Slow Civil War* (New York: W.W. Norton & Company, 2023), 187.
8. "'First-Ever' Evangelical Conference on Transgender Issues Set for Oct. 5 in Louisville," Southern Baptist Theological Seminary, accessed March 14, 2025, https://www.sbts.edu/news/first-ever-evangelical-conference-on-transgender-issues-set-for-oct-5-in-louisville/.
9. Zane McNeill, "Republicans Spent Nearly $215M on TV Ads Attacking Trans Rights This Election," Truthout, November 5, 2024, https://truthout.org/articles/republicans-spent-nearly-215m-on-tv-ads-attacking-trans-rights-this-election/.
10. While 2 percent of the American population identifies as transgender, that percentage increases when adjusting for generational populations. Anna Brown, "About 5% of Young Adults in the U.S. Say Their Gender Is Different from Their Sex Assigned at Birth," Pew Research Center (blog), June 7, 2022, https://www.pewresearch.org/short-reads/2022/06/07/about-5-of-young-adults-in-the-u-s-say-their-gender-is-different-from-their-sex-assigned-at-birth/.
11. Joseph Gedeon, "US Justice Department Removes Study Finding Far-Right Extremists Commit 'Far More' Violence," *The Guardian*, September 17, 2025, https://www.theguardian.com/us-news/2025/sep/17/justice-department-study-far-right-extremist-violence.
12. ABPnews, "'20/20' Investigates Sexual Abuse in SBC, Other Protestant Bodies," Baptist News Global, April 15, 2007, https://baptistnews.com/article/20-20-investigates-sexual-abuse-in-sbc-other-protestant-bodies/.
13. Robert Downen, Lise Olsen, and John Tedesco, "20 Years, 700 Victims: Southern Baptist Sexual Abuse Spreads as Leaders Resist Reforms," *Houston Chronicle*, February 10, 2019, https://www.houstonchronicle.com/news/investigations/article/Southern-Baptist-sexual-abuse-spreads-as-leaders-13588038.php.
14. Bob Smietana—Religion News Service, "Southern Baptists Abandon Abuse Database," *Christianity Today*, February 19, 2025, https://www.christianitytoday.com/2025/02/southern-baptist-abuse-database-pastors-ec-sbc/.
15. Scott Barkley, "Iorg Addresses Sexual Abuse, Financial Realities in

Report to Executive Committee," Baptist Press, February 17, 2025, https://www.baptistpress.com/resource-library/news/iorg-addresses-sexual-abuse-financial-realities-in-report-to-executive-committee/.
16. Denny Burk (@DennyBurk), "So here's bottom line on the SBC abuse 'crisis.' There wasn't one. A federal investigation closed after making one arrest—not for abuse but for making false statements under oath. An independent investigation by Guidepost Solutions found no systemic problem with abuse at the SBC Executive Committee," X (formerly Twitter), March 12, 2025, https://x.com/DennyBurk/status/1899904896734007337.
17. Aleksandr Solzhenitsyn, "Nobel Lecture," trans. Alexis Klimoff, Aleksandr Solzhenitsyn Center, August 3, 2023, https://www.solzhenitsyncenter.org/nobel-lecture.
18. Sander van der Linden and Lee C. McIntyre, "How to Address Misinformation—Without Censorship," *Time*, May 6, 2025, https://time.com/7282640/how-to-address-misinformation/.
19. David Harsanyi, *The Rise of BlueAnon: How the Democrats Became a Party of Conspiracy Theorists* (New York: Broadside Books, 2024).
20. Eberhard Bethge, "A Visit to Thomas Road Church," *The Wild Goose* (1:2), July 1990, 15–16.
21. Frederick Douglass, *Narrative of the Life of Frederick Douglass, an American Slave*, First Edition (Boston, MA: Anti-Slavery Office, 1845), 118–19.
22. Walter Brueggemann, *Reality, Grief, Hope: Three Urgent Prophetic Tasks* (Grand Rapids, MI: Wm. B. Eerdmans Publishing Co., 2014).

Chapter 3: An Untold Story

1. Richard Hofstadter, *Anti-Intellectualism in American Life* (New York: Vintage Books, 1963), 47.
2. Bebbington conceived of the quadrilateral as a concept applied for his history of evangelical Christianity in the UK. But the quadrilateral got to be so popular it basically became the industry standard for historians and more academically inclined evangelicals who wanted to define and describe their identity. But there's a slew of problems with the quadrilateral. One is obvious: most people have no idea it exists as an academic concept. But there are other problems, too.

Daniel Silliman, who was an editor for the evangelical flagship magazine, *Christianity Today*, realized that when he examined all the historical decisions that went into the founding of *Christianity Today*, not one of the theological beliefs explained why the founders of *CT* drew the lines they did, keeping some people out (like C. S. Lewis) and inviting others in (like W. B. Criswell, a pro-segregation pastor of First Baptist Dallas, where current pastor Robert Jeffress vocalizes support for Trump).

3. Daniel Silliman, "An Evangelical Is Anyone Who Likes Billy Graham: Defining Evangelicalism with Carl Henry and Networks of Trust," *Church History* 90, no. 3 (September 2021): 621–43, https://doi.org/10.1017/S000964072100216X.

4. Sociologist Ryan Burge talks about this shift here: Ryan Burge, "The Rise of the Non-Christian Evangelical," Graphs About Religion, Substack, February 26, 2024, https://substack.com/home/post/p-141364618.

5. Michael Butter, "Mapping American Conspiracism," in *Plots, Designs, and Schemes: American Conspiracy Theories from the Puritans to the Present* (Boston, MA: De Gruyter, Inc., 2014), 51.

6. Cotton Mather and Increase Mather, *The Wonders of the Invisible World Being an Account of the Tryals of Several Witches Lately Executed in New-England, to Which Is Added a Farther Account of the Tryals of the New-England Witches* (Project Gutenberg [2009], 1693), 13–14.

7. Mather and Mather, *The Wonders of the Invisible World*, vi–vii. 42.

8. Mather and Mather, *The Wonders of the Invisible World*, vi–vii.

9. Mather and Mather, *The Wonders of the Invisible World*, viii.

10. Mather and Mather, *The Wonders of the Invisible World*, vi.

11. Mather and Mather, *The Wonders of the Invisible World*, 5.

12. Mather and Mather, *The Wonders of the Invisible World*, 10–11.

13. "And by the Presence and Power of the Divine Institutions thus maintained in the Country, We are still so happy, that I supposed there is no Land in the Universe more free from the debauching, and the debasing Vices of Ungodliness." Mather and Mather, *The Wonders of the Invisible World*, 11.

14. Frank Lambert, *Inventing the "Great Awakening"* (Princeton, NJ: Princeton University Press, 2001).

15. Andrew F. Walls, *The Missionary Movement in Christian History:*

Studies in the Transmission of Faith (Maryknoll, NY; Edinburgh: Orbis Books; T&T Clark, 1996), 82–84.

16. Now, evangelical Christianity the world over has, in certain contexts, jettisoned the assumption of Christian supremacy. Evangelical Christians worship in Palestine, Myanmar, and India—places where the possibility of political dominance is not readily entertained or assumed.
17. Lambert, *Inventing the "Great Awakening,"* 15–16.
18. John Gillies, *Memoirs of the Life of the Reverend George Whitefield, ... Faithfully Selected from His Original Papers, Journals, and Letters.... Compiled by the Rev. John Gillies, D.D.*, Eighteenth Century Collections Online (London: printed for Edward and Charles Dilly; and Messieurs Kincaid and Creech, at Edinburgh, 1772), 137.
19. One notable divergence is the stream of evangelical universalism traced in the work of Robin Parry and recounted in David W. Congdon, ed., *Varieties of Christian Universalism: Exploring Four Views* (Grand Rapids, MI: Baker Academic, 2023).
20. Charles F. Irons, *The Origins of Proslavery Christianity: White and Black Evangelicals in Colonial and Antebellum Virginia* (Chapel Hill: University of North Carolina Press, 2008), 35.
21. John MacArthur, "Who's to Blame for the Riots?," Grace to You, accessed September 25, 2023, https://www.gty.org/sermons/81-80/whos-to-blame-for-the-riots.
22. "Our Augusta Letter," *Atlanta Constitution*, May 4, 1876.
23. Edward J. Blum and John Stauffer, *Reforming the White Republic: Race, Religion, and American Nationalism, 1865–1989*, First Edition (Baton Rouge: LSU Press, 2007).
24. Matthew Avery Sutton, *American Apocalypse: A History of Modern Evangelicalism* (Cambridge, MA: Harvard University Press, 2014), 173.
25. M. A. Matthews, "Interview in re Our National Duty," Sermonettes 1917, box 16, accession 97-2, MAM; Billy Sunday, *Face to Face with Satan* (Knoxville, TN: Prudential Publishing, 1923), 75. See also "Our Immigration Problem," CWM (September 1914), 14–15, cited in Sutton, *American Apocalypse*, 123.
26. "Despite fundamentalist talk of doctrinal purity as the foundation for Christian fellowship, the color line always trumped theology." Sutton, *American Apocalypse*, 109.

27. Sutton, *American Apocalypse*, 125.
28. Sutton, *American Apocalypse*, 129.
29. Sutton, *American Apocalypse*, 121.
30. Axel R. Schäfer, *Piety and Public Funding: Evangelicals and the State in Modern America*, First Edition, Politics and Culture in Modern America (Philadelphia, PA: University of Pennsylvania Press, 2012).
31. J. Frank Norris, "The Second Coming of Christ," SermonIndex, accessed January 24, 2025, https://www.sermonindex.net/sermons/aayzZlMDSwHvUIUV.
32. Thomas Mallon, "A View from the Fringe," *The New Yorker*, January 3, 2016, https://www.newyorker.com/magazine/2016/01/11/a-view-from-the-fringe.
33. Matthew Dallek, *Birchers: How the John Birch Society Radicalized the American Right* (New York: Basic Books, 2023), 58.
34. Dallek, *Birchers*, 56.
35. Dallek, *Birchers*, 77.
36. Silliman, "An Evangelical Is Anyone Who Likes Billy Graham," 637.
37. Silliman, "An Evangelical Is Anyone Who Likes Billy Graham," 637.
38. "Conservative Book Club Advertisement," *Christianity Today*, January 7, 1966, 56.
39. Lee Edwards and Anne Edwards, "How Publishers Learned to Love Conservative Books," *Daily Signal*, April 13, 2015, https://www.dailysignal.com/2015/04/13/how-publishers-and-readers-learned-to-love-conservative-books/.
40. "Conservative Book Club Advertisement," *Christianity Today*, January 7, 1966, 56.
41. See "Eutychus and His Kin," *Christianity Today*, February 4, 1966, https://www.christianitytoday.com/1966/02/eutychus-and-his-kin-232/; "Eutychus and His Kin," *Christianity Today*, March 4, 1966, https://www.christianitytoday.com/1966/03/eutychus-and-his-kin-234/.
42. See "Eutychus and His Kin," *Christianity Today*, February 4, 1966, and "Eutychus and His Kin" *Christianity Today*, March 4, 1966.
43. "Eutychus and His Kin," *Christianity Today*, February 4, 1966, 43.
44. "Eutychus and His Kin," *Christianity Today*, February 4, 1966, 43.
45. "Conversation 662-004," Richard Nixon Museum and Library, n.d.

46. "Conversation 662-004," Richard Nixon Museum and Library, Marker: 1:05:45.
47. Tim LaHaye, *Rapture (Under Attack): Will You Escape the Tribulation?* (Multnomah Books, 1998), 138.
48. Daniel G. Hummel, *The Rise and Fall of Dispensationalism: How the Evangelical Battle over the End Times Shaped a Nation* (Grand Rapids, MI: Wm. B. Eerdmans Publishing Co., 2023), 474–75.
49. Jerry B. Jenkins and Tim LaHaye, *The Vanishings (Left Behind: The Kids)* (Wheaton, IL: Tyndale House Publishers, 1998).
50. Anne Nelson, *Shadow Network: Media, Money, and the Secret Hub of the Radical Right* (New York: Bloomsbury Publishing, 2019).
51. Some readers may confuse material network analysis into the CNP for a baseless left-coded conspiracy theory. This would be a dangerous mistake for two reasons. First, generally, material network analysis meets the burden of evidence in ways conspiracy theory never does. Second, specifically, it risks normalizing now-pardoned CNP-associated actors who diverged from best practices that characterize democracy-aligned policy institutions with their documented attempts to interfere in a free election in 2020. All in the name of "election integrity.".
52. United States Federal Communications Commission, "FCC Record, Volume 2, No. 17, Pages 5002 to 5398, August 17–August 28, 1987," book, UNT Digital Library (United States Government Printing Office, August 1987).
53. Christopher H. Sterling, Cary O'Dell, and Michael C. Keith, eds., "Rush Limbaugh," in *The Biographical Encyclopedia of American Radio*, Concise and rev. ed. (New York: Routledge, 2011), 233–35.
54. Nelson, *Shadow Network*, 54–55.
55. "Conservative Media," Salem Media, October 28, 2025, https://salemmedia.com/conservative-media.
56. "Recordings and Materials from Council for National Policy Meetings," Documented, accessed June 19, 2023, https://documented.net/investigations/council-for-national-policy-recordings.
57. Powell was instrumental in filing legal challenges asserting election fraud in the weeks following the presidential election, challenges that were legally declared "baseless" and resulted in an Appeals Court upholding. See King et al. v. Whitmer et al., No. 21–1785 (United States Court of Appeals, 6th Circuit, June 23, 2023).

58. "CNP October 2019 Panel—Fitton, Page, Powell," Vimeo, posted October 21, 2020, by documented.net, https://vimeo.com/470515497.
59. "CNP October 2019 Panel—Fitton, Page, Powell," Vimeo.
60. "CNP October 2019 Panel—Fitton, Page, Powell," Vimeo.
61. Charlie Kirk (@charliekirk11), "RT if the Senate should ACT and fight back against Democrats' deep state coup!" Twitter, October 17, 2019, https://twitter.com/charliekirk11/status/1184995611487039488.
62. Charlie Kirk (@charliekirk11), "Voter fraud is real," Twitter, November 28, 2020, https://twitter.com/charliekirk11/status/1332838620756000769.
63. Charlie Kirk (@charliekirk11), "There is more evidence of systemic voter fraud in America than 'systemic racism' yet which one do you think Democrats are more worried about?" Twitter, December 4, 2020, https://twitter.com/charliekirk11/status/1334934358114718 72.
64. Stanley Hauerwas, *The Peaceable Kingdom: A Primer in Christian Ethics* (Notre Dame, IN: University of Notre Dame Press, 1983), 70.

Chapter 4: The Plot Devices of Holy Paranoia

1. Spotsylvania Conservative Women, "March for TRUMP 1/6," Facebook, accessed November 15, 2023, https://archive.is/NrKXj.
2. Franklin Graham (@Franklin_Graham), "Join me in praying that if there is fraud, it would be proven—for the good of our nation & all future elections. Forces of evil are at work, & we know how much is at stake. Pray for God's will to be done in the outcome of this important election," Twitter, December 8, 2020, https://twitter.com/Franklin_Graham/status/1336386265596440583.
3. Eric Metaxas (@ericmetaxas), "Those criticizing the Jericho March gathering in DC are straining at a gnat to swallow a camel. Where is the outrage at those who would dare to steal an election? Where is the call for transparency & investigation? Those of us gathered were there to pray that God would intervene," Twitter, December 17, 2020, https://twitter.com/ericmetaxas/status/1339560090790227974.
4. Tony Perkins (@tperkins), "Join us as we pray for election integrity in Georgia and that Georgians will elect candidates to the U.S. Senate who will uphold the sanctity of all human life and protect our nation's fundamental freedoms. LIVE: http://Prayvotestand

.Org," Twitter, December 17, 2020, https://x.com/tperkins/status/1339376610265456643.
5. Paula White-Cain (@Paula_White), "I ask you to pray fervently, without ceasing for our nation and the election results. There is great concern that some are trying to steal this election. Let us pray to God, who knows all, to reveal truth. Pray that the enemies to God are quieted and their plans are overturned," Twitter, November 4, 2020, https://twitter.com/Paula_White/status/1324074690168692738.
6. Naomi Klein and Astra Taylor, "The Rise of End Times Fascism," *The Guardian*, April 13, 2025, sec. US news, https://www.theguardian.com/us-news/ng-interactive/2025/apr/13/end-times-fascism-far-right-trump-musk.
7. Augustine, *City of God*, volume VI, books 18.36–20, Loeb Classical Library (Cambridge, MA: Harvard University Press, 1960), 360–61.
8. Ellul, *To Will & To Do: An Introduction to Christian Ethics*, Volume I, trans. Jacob Marques Rollison (Eugene, OR: Cascade Books, 2020), Loc. 4407, Kindle.
9. Isaiah 11:6.
10. Timothy Melley, *Empire of Conspiracy: The Culture of Paranoia in Postwar America* (Ithaca, NY: Cornell University Press, 2016), 6, Kindle.
11. Jürgen Moltmann, *An Introduction to Christian Theology*, ed. Douglas Meeks (Durham, NC: Duke, 1968), 30–31.
12. "Papers of Howard Thurman | 'The Fascist Masquerade,' 1946," The Howard Thurman Papers Project, accessed May 10, 2025, https://thurmanpapersproject.org/documents/820.
13. Manichaeism developed in the third century CE in Persia. It combined elements of Christian and pagan sources, and held to a view of history that saw an ongoing battle between light and darkness. See John F. Matthews, "Manichaeism," *Oxford Classical Dictionary*, July 30, 2015, accessed May 19, 2025, https://oxfordre.com/classics/view/10.1093/acrefore/9780199381135.001.0001/acrefore-9780199381135-e-3914.
14. Tragically, the practice of adoption is also inverted with great damage, transformed into a service *by* children *for* parents.
15. Ephesians 1:5.
16. Ulrich, *Transfigured not Conformed*, 261.
17. Ellul, *To Will & To Do*, 118.
18. Ellul, *To Will & To Do*, 189.

19. Brian Brock, *Captive to Christ, Open to the World: On Doing Christian Ethics in Public*, ed. Kenneth Oakes (Eugene, OR: Cascade Books, 2014), 55.
20. "Pentagon AI More Ethical Because of 'Judeo-Christian' Roots Will Ensure U.S. Military AI Is Used Ethically," *Washington Post*, July 26, 2023, https://www.washingtonpost.com/national-security/2023/07/22/air-force-general-ai-judeochristian/.
21. To read more on how "worship" and the Christian ethos are bound up together, see Ulrich, *Transfigured not Conformed*, 71.
22. I Peter 4:13.
23. Alberto Toscano, *Late Fascism: Race, Capitalism and the Politics of Crisis* (London and New York: Verso Books, 2023), 94.
24. Dietrich Bonhoeffer and Victoria Barnett, *Theological Education Underground, 1937–1940*, Dietrich Bonhoeffer Works, Vol. 15 (Minneapolis: Fortress Press, 2011), 194.

Chapter 5: Red-Pilled Evangelicalism

1. Conspiracism has no ideological home. It is present on the political left *and* right. But confronting conspiracism in evangelicalism inevitably leads us to the right.
2. Stanley Hauerwas, *Fully Alive: The Apocalyptic Humanism of Karl Barth*, Richard E. Myers Lectures (Charlottesville: University of Virginia Press, 2022), 119–21.
3. Chip Rotolo, "White Evangelicals Continue to Stand Out in Their Support for Trump," *Pew Research Center* (blog), April 28, 2025, https://www.pewresearch.org/short-reads/2025/04/28/white-evangelicals-continue-to-stand-out-in-their-support-for-trump/.
4. Rotolo, "White Evangelicals Continue to Stand Out in Their Support for Trump."
5. Liz Charlotte Grant, "The Certainty Summit," *The Christian Century*, March 13, 2025, https://www.christiancentury.org/features/certainty-summit.
6. Jack Jenkins, "Jan. 6: A Timeline in Prayers," *Interfaith America* (blog), January 6, 2022, https://www.interfaithamerica.org/article/jan-6-a-timeline-in-prayers/.
7. Jude Joffe-Block, "Four Years After the Capitol Riot, Why QAnon Hasn't

Gone Away," NPR, *Morning Edition*, December 30, 2024, https://www.npr.org/2024/12/30/nx-s1-5230801/qanon-capitol-riot-social-media.
8. PRRI, "The Persistence of QAnon in the Post-Trump Era."
9. Dietrich Bonhoeffer, *God Is in the Manger: Reflections on Advent and Christmas* (Louisville, KY: Westminster John Knox Press, 2012), 80.
10. Quinn Slobodian, *Crack-Up Capitalism: Market Radicals and the Dream of a World Without Democracy* (New York: Metropolitan Books, 2023), Loc. 220, Kindle.
11. Slobodian, *Crack-Up Capitalism*, Loc. 113.

Chapter 6: Claimed by Reality

1. Graham Greene, *Our Man in Havana* (Penguin Classics, 2007).
2. James Baldwin, "AS MUCH TRUTH AS ONE CAN BEAR; To Speak Out About the World as It Is, Says James Baldwin, Is the Writer's Job As Much of the Truth as One Can Bear," *New York Times*, January 14, 1962, https://www.nytimes.com/1962/01/14/archives/as-much-truth-as-one-can-bear-to-speak-out-about-the-world-as-it-is.html.
3. Baldwin, "AS MUCH TRUTH AS ONE CAN BEAR."
4. James 3:1–12.
5. Anna Dorn, "The Medium Newsletter: How Names Shape Reality," Medium, June 17, 2025, https://medium.com/blog/how-names-shape-reality-4c1b5e1e6510.
6. Serge Brédart, "The Cognitive Psychology and Neuroscience of Naming People," *Neuroscience & Biobehavioral Reviews* 83 (December 1, 2017): 145–54, https://doi.org/10.1016/j.neubiorev.2017.10.008.
7. Theologian David Bentley Hart is talking about God right on the borders of these fascinating developments: "Whatever the nature of matter may be" he argues, "the primal reality of all things is mind." See David Bentley Hart, *All Things Are Full of Gods: The Mysteries of Mind and Life* (New Haven, CT: Yale University Press, 2024), 66.
8. I am indebted to Brian Brock for this reading of Genesis and naming. See more in Brian Brock, *Joining Creation's Praise* (Baylor, TX: Baylor Press, 2025).
9. John 1:1–14.
10. Aleksandr Solzhenitsyn, "Nobel Lecture."
11. John 18:37.

12. Friedrich Nietzsche, *Beyond Good and Evil*, trans. Helen Zimmern (Classicbooks by KTHTK, 2018).
13. Scott Detrow, host, *All Things Considered*, podcast, "Russell Moore on 'an Altar Call' for Evangelical America," NPR, August 5, 2023, https://www.npr.org/2023/08/05/1192374014/russell-moore-on-altar-call-for-evangelical-america.
14. LeaveReligion, "James River Men's Conference Madness," reddit, April 29, 2023, https://www.reddit.com/r/springfieldMO/comments/132kckm/james_river_mens_conference_madness/?rdt=63118.
15. For example, Chad Williams is a former SEAL who has spoken at First Baptist Dallas where Senior Pastor Robert Jeffress, who has a decade of association with Donald Trump, offered his endorsement: "Every year we select a special guest speaker who models both a love for God and a love for our great country; and we could not have selected a better guest.... He's got a compelling story, he is one of the very few people I want to hear a second time!" https://www.sealofchrist.com/bio.
16. Garrett Unclebach (@garrettunclebach), "Men must be CAPABLE of violence. #discipline #mindset #men #christian #strength #navyseals #military #inspiration #reels," Instagram, January 27, 2023, https://www.instagram.com/reel/Cn72knxvH4N/.
17. Media Posts by Elon Musk (@elonmusk) / X, X (formerly Twitter), March 16, 2025, https://x.com/elonmusk.
18. Stan Goff, *Borderline: Reflections on War, Sex, and Church* (Eugene, OR: Cascade Books, 2015), 1.
19. ASMR stands for "autonomous sensory meridian response," and it's a sort of digital content that emphasizes auditory sensations that, basically, give people the goose bumps. The Trump White House created an ASMR video of people in chains being deported onto planes. The videos used the clanking metallic sounds of chains and handcuffs as part of its deportation propaganda.
20. Michael Wyschogrod, *The Body of Faith: God in the People Israel* (Northvale, NJ: Rowman & Littlefield Publishers, Inc., 2000).
21. Eve Upton-Clark, "Pentagon Pizza Index: The Theory That Surging Pizza Orders Signal Global Crises," *Fast Company*, June 16, 2025, https://www.fastcompany.com/91352935/pentagon-pizza-index-the-theory-that-surging-pizza-orders-signal-global-crises.
22. John Steinbeck, *The Grapes of Wrath* in *The Complete Works of John Steinbeck* (Hastings, UK: Delphi, 1939), Loc. 19059, Kindle.

23. K. H. Miskotte, *Biblical ABCs: The Basics of Christian Resistance*, trans. Eleonora Hof and Collin Cornell (Lanham, MD: Fortress Academic, 2023), 19.
24. Cody Bivins-Starr, "Transfiguring Madness: A Messianic-Apocalyptic Theological Account of Psychotic Experience," PhD dissertation, University of Aberdeen, School of Divinity, 2025.
25. Brian Brock, *Captive to Christ, Open to the World: On Doing Christian Ethics in Public*, ed. by Kenneth Oakes (Eugene, OR: Cascade Books, 2014).
26. Acts 17:28–29.
27. Abraham Heschel, "The Holy Dimension." *Journal of Religion* 23, no. 2 (April 1943): 117–24, https://doi.org/10.1086/482993.
28. David Bentley Hart, "Tradition and Disruption," *Plough*, June 3, 2022, https://www.plough.com/en/topics/faith/early-christians/tradition-and-disruption.
29. I am indebted to Brian Brock for this observation. See Brian Brock, *Captive to Christ, Open to the World*, 125.

Chapter 7: Toward a Common World

1. On the idea of better politics as being downriver of becoming better people, see Michael R. Wear's excellent book *The Spirit of Our Politics: Spiritual Formation and the Renovation of Public Life* (Grand Rapids, MI: Zondervan, 2024).
2. Hello, fellow grammar nerds! The Latin past participle *suspicere* communicates a posture, "to look up at." You could imagine someone looking "up" at the gods with a mixture of ignorance and fear. See "Suspicion | Etymology of Suspicion," Etymonline, accessed January 20, 2025, https://www.etymonline.com/word/suspicion.
3. "Suspicion | Etymology of Suspicion."
4. It's also true that *Casablanca* started shooting before the script was finished. They wrote the film as they shot it.
5. Jason Blakely, *Lost in Ideology: Interpreting Modern Political Life* (Newcastle upon Tyne, UK: Agenda Publishing, 2024), 3.
6. Blakely, *Lost in Ideology*, 1.
7. David Bentley Hart, "Mammon Ascendant," *First Things*, June 1, 2016, https://www.firstthings.com/article/2016/06/mammon-ascendant.

8. We often think of the word "closed-minded" to refer to backward thinking, to "being out of step with history." But this, too, is an ideological read! The assumption that history is only ever *progress*, something that cannot *regress* or diverge from a ceaseless march toward enlightenment.
9. Acts 10:34.
10. Eugene Peterson, *The Message: The Bible in Contemporary Language* (NavPress, 2023).
11. 1 Peter 4:17.
12. Hans Günter Ulrich, *Transfigured Not Conformed: Christian Ethics in a Hermeneutic Key*, ed. Brian Brock (London: T&T Clark, 2021), 120.
13. Ernst Käsemann and James Cone, *Church Conflicts: The Cross, Apocalyptic, and Political Resistance*, ed. Ry Siggelkow, trans. Roy A. Harrisville (Grand Rapids, MI: Baker Academic, 2021), 216.
14. Helon Kenyon, "Worship Hour Found Time of Segregation," *New York Times*, November 4, 1952, https://www.nytimes.com/1952/11/04/archives/worship-hour-found-time-of-segregation.html.
15. McGavran would write, "The principle I am setting forth, which plays such a large part in the growth of the church, should not be understood as condoning white racial pride. Nothing I have said justifies injustice and intolerance, or the strong enforcing segregation on the weak. . . . If class distinctions continue, they do so in spite of the Christian faith, not because of it." Donald A. McGavran and C. Peter Wagner, *Understanding Church Growth*, Third Edition (Grand Rapids, MI: W.B. Eerdmans, 1990), 169.
16. Jesse Curtis, "White Evangelicals as a 'People': The Church Growth Movement from India to the United States," *Religion and Culture* 30, no. 1 (2020): 134.

Chapter 8: Sand in the Machine

1. Willie James Jennings, *Acts: A Theological Commentary on the Bible (Belief: A Theological Commentary on the Bible)* (Louisville, KY: Presbyterian Publishing Corporation, 2017), 45–46, Kindle.
2. John 3:8.
3. Mark 3:31–34.
4. John 14:6.